QUESTIONS THAT A WOMAN HAS
TO ANSWER:

How do tax laws discriminate against women?

What happens to a woman's joint savings account
when her husband dies?

What fine print does a woman have to read carefully in insurance policies?

What are the different paths to retirement security?

How long do you have to keep financial records to
satisfy the government?

How do you protect your financial interests in a
divorce?

When should a woman be suspicious of a lawyer
or a broker?

When is the best time to take investment risks?

Where are the best places to look for high interest
on your savings?

*In this splendid guide you will be able to find the
answer to every question that concerns you—and
do it with amazing swiftness and complete satis-
faction. Never before has so much vital information been made so readily available!*

ABOUT THE AUTHORS

GUSTAVE SIMONS, eminent tax attorney and noted financial authority, is the author of two widely acclaimed books on financial planning for women—*What Every Woman Doesn't Know,* and *Coping with Crisis.* His wife, ALICE SIMONS, is founder of the Weston Workshop for Women, and leader of its five-year study of the role of women in contemporary society.

MONEY AND WOMEN

by

Gustave and Alice Simons

POPULAR LIBRARY • NEW YORK

MONEY AND WOMEN

Published by Popular Library, a unit of CBS Publications, the Consumer Publishing Division of CBS Inc.

ISBN: 0-445-04394-6

Printed in the United States of America

10   9   8   7   6   5   4   3   2   1

Contents

Introduction

Money and Women says: "Women *can* count." At least as well as husbands or other men in their economic lives. Yet most women—single, married, divorced, or widowed, and of all ages—need new confidence if they are to escape financial slavery and become equal partners with men in the world of personal finance. They must make the effort to become *women who count*.

No mysterious training is needed for competent money management beyond eighth-grade mathematics and an inquiring mind. But the modern tragedy is that women still do not believe themselves and their ability to count. "I wish" has not become "I will."

This book, written by Gustave and Alice Winslow Simons offers women an informed approach to all areas of their personal finances—before it's too late.

Money and Women is a how-to-do-it book directed toward the financially unsophisticated woman. Women do most of the spending of the nation's money, much of the earning (roughly 50 percent of women over sixteen are in the labor market) and a good part of the saving.

She is the beneficiary of most of the life insurance and owns a great share of the country's real estate. Though considerable money passes through her hands, she lacks information about record keeping, taxation, estate planning, insurance, investments, and banking. This knowledge will help to make her an active participant rather than a passive recipient. Without such knowledge—and the power it generates—liberation of women is meaningless.

In 1964, Gustave Simons, tax attorney and fiscal expert, published *What Every Woman Doesn't Know,* a serious work on financial planning for women. In 1972, his second book *Coping with Crisis* was based on many of the dilemmas and problems women face. *Money and Women* is his third book in the field, this time coauthored with his wife Alice, founder of the Weston Workshop for Women and leader of its five-year study of the role of women in contemporary society.

The authors believe it is critical for women to learn to ask the significant questions and to find the right answers. Example? The establishment of credit (with banks, department stores, and brokers) has been extremely difficult for women. Yet how many have taken the time or the proper steps to demand their rights under the new Equal Credit Opportunity Act?

On the other side, the authors say that the way to avoid many financial pitfalls is to know when and how to seek expert advice. The do-it-herself woman with the free services of a brother-in-law is only too likely to make a mess of an investment program—let alone a will.

Although this book is primarily directed toward women it must be emphasized that much of the material can be of equal or even greater importance to men. For example a good pension plan is of equal, or even greater importance, to a woman's husband, father, son, brother, or housemate. Since women usually have a longer life expectancy than the men in their lives, the chapters on Inheritance (chapter 9) and Life Insurance (chapter 7) are of critical importance, not only with regard to wills that women make and life insurance that they purchase for the benefit of others, but to wills and life insurance with which their husbands or fathers may be involved.

As the book evolved, it became increasingly evident that in most of the chapters, two of the most important aspects of the material were to inform the reader when to *call* for professional help and, even more important and more difficult, how to *select* the best available professional help. Any attorney or financial adviser finds that the identification of competent and honest experts and the making of appropriate financial arrangements with them is often the most important and difficult aspect of financial planning. Accordingly, the last chapter in the book has been devoted to this subject and will review the way to find and evaluate the most appropriate expert.

Before settling into chapter 1 the reader might want to test herself on the following questions. Even this short list reveals how *Money and Women* may serve to help women achieve a giant leap toward financial freedom.

1. Do you have a dead-end job?
2. How do you evaluate the fringe benefits that go with your job?
3. What is a tax shelter?
4. What are the most effective tax shelters today?
5. How do tax laws discriminate against women?
6. How do you plan to fund your retirement?
7. How do you plan to fund the education of your children?
8. Have you begun to think about estate planning? What steps have you taken?
9. What is a "living trust"?

10. What are the advantages of a "living trust"?
11. Why and when is life insurance subject to an estate tax? Can this burden be avoided?
12. How do you plan for the financial future of your children?
13. How can you provide lifetime security for a married daughter at minimum cost?
14. In what state can the least expensive insurance be purchased?
15. Is it possible to make life insurance costs tax deductible?
16. How do you decide how much and what kind of insurance your family requires?
17. How do you select a reliable and effective insurance company?
18. Is real estate a good investment?
19. How do you start a new business with the best financial protection?
20. What kinds of personal records should be kept? For how long?
21. What are the advantages and risks of joint tax returns?
22. Should you invest in the stock market? When?
23. What happens to community property on the death of a wife or husband?
24. How do you select lawyers, accountants, bankers, and other advisers?

1
Recording It

Record keeping is essential in today's complicated world. Part of the complexity lies in the vast quantity of paper that sifts over the land like a perpetual snowstorm. Each mail brings advertisements, solicitations, banking communications, periodicals, personal letters, bills, and sometimes even a welcome check. To sort, to decide what to keep and what to throw away, what course of action to take, and where and how to keep needed papers has become a major part of personal and business life. In most matters financial, it is not enough to remember: you must have proof. There is nothing more frustrating than to require a particular document and not be able to find it. Keeping track is therefore the first essential task. Papers must be readily available, transportable intact from one location to another, storable in a space that leaves room for expansion, and clearly labeled and indexed.

Every woman, whether she is married, single, divorced, widowed, salaried, or nonsalaried, who wants to be in charge of her own life, must learn to keep records. It's especially essential for women because there are so many changes in most women's lives; they may play many roles, sometimes all together, and may live in many places and work at different jobs. A woman may start out with no more than the baby-sitting money in her jeans and end up with a house (rented or owned), condominium, boat, vacation home, or all of them. She may live alone, then marry, then have children. Whatever her status, she should make a plan *now*. (Remember, it is never too late to begin.) It may seem like a headache, but it's essential. Whenever a job is distasteful, learn to do it superlatively well in order to get it done as quickly as possible.

The way to start is to anticipate the snowstorm of paper and be ready with places for everything. The records may fit into a few labeled envelopes or may require a desk, filing cabinet, storage closet, portable strongbox, and safe deposit box, but everything should be easily available. Important documents should be quickly portable (as in case of fire) and space should be ample to allow for expansion. In addition to labeling everything clearly it is very helpful to have an index box of three-by-five inch cards on which are noted information about vital papers and where they may be found. For example, one card should list the contents of the safe deposit box. Another should list all insurance policies and their location. A third should carry banking information. And so on.

The items that should constitute records are usually in five categories, as follows:

1. *Current Matters*
   Checkbooks
   Bank statements
   Canceled checks
   Paid bills
   Unpaid bills
   Most recent tax returns
   Information for tax returns

Education records
Employment records
Guarantees and proofs of purchase of goods
under warranty
Charge card itemized statements
Professional correspondence on financial
matters

2. *Former Years*
Bank statements
Bankbooks
Canceled checks
Paid bills
Tax returns for all former years
Tax backup material for past seven years
Charge card statements

3. *Vital Papers*
Birth certificate
Citizenship papers
Name changes
Marriage certificate
Divorce decree
Adoption papers
Deeds
Mortgages
Auto titles
Stock certificates
Bonds
Military discharge
Proof as to amount and date of purchase of
assets over $1,000

4. *Urgent* (On hand for immediate use as neces-
sary)
Insurance policies
Inventories
Passports
Savings passbooks

      Leases
      Contracts
      Wills
      Trusts
      Licenses
      Safe deposit box key
      Filing cabinet key

5. *Valuables* (i.e., important capital assets)
      Jewelry
      Coin collections
      Stamp collections
      First editions and rare books
      Original works of art
      Antiques

Each of these five categories should have a special place. *Current Matters* should be easily available in whatever spot you choose to make your financial management center. Most women's magazines show pictures of "planning centers" for women. Usually they are shown tucked into a corner of the kitchen, or into a recess in a hall, and are tastefully decorated with a wicker basket of yarn and a gourmet cookbook or two. But they are never large enough. The notion that women need to keep complete financial records has not so far found its way into the minds of home designers. Yet a business center in a home is as important as a linen closet. Incidentally the housewife who sets up an office of her own for conducting all phases of home management, including financial, may gain an odd extra advantage: she may find that her status in the home goes up several notches. This is visible proof that she considers herself a professional in her job as homemaker, and not a second-class citizen, unpaid, unappreciated, unskilled.

For the woman living alone, record keeping may take up no more than a corner. But it will be a *cornerstone* of financial sanity. Whatever the size, a businesslike approach to personal financial management will not only make money go farther, it will make a better life possible.

Day-to-day records must go into filing folders. Each folder should have a year and a name clearly marked. This avoids lumping everything together, which will result in an enormous job of sorting out what to keep for permanent records and what to discard.

Take, for example, the papers that may be required to back up assertions on tax returns. These need be kept only six years from the date of filing. To take care of late filing, we recommend keeping tax backup material for seven years. Up to that time a tax return may be questioned by the government and the taxpayer must furnish proof of statements made. After that time, most tax backup material may be safely discarded, always excepting the case of deliberate fraud. There is no time limitation on fraud; the Internal Revenue Service can investigate fraud any time, even many years later. Normally, it is good filing practice to place all tax backup material for a particular year in one folder so that at the end of the seven-year period all *but* material needed to prove cost and date of acquisition of important capital assets or to record important transactions may be discarded.

Examples of Folders for Current Matters

> TAX BACKUP MATERIAL (YEAR)
> Receipts for interest paid, purchases of real estate, purchases of expensive equipment
> Medical expenses
> Lists of persons entertained for business
> Thank-you notes from business persons entertained
> Dividend notices
> W-2 forms
> (Check with your accountant for other items you should keep. If you take the standard

deduction, you will not need to itemize some of the above.)

BANKING: NAME OF BANK AND YEAR
Statements
Canceled checks
Deposit slips
Completed checkbooks

PAID BILLS (YEAR)
At the end of the year take your current bill file and remove bills that are not necessary for the tax backup file. There may be personal reasons for keeping some old bills, but not tax reasons. Clip canceled checks to the bills that are kept, whenever possible.

LAST YEAR'S INCOME TAX RETURN
Make up a folder for your copy of last year's income tax return. Keep it with *Current Matters* until the original is filed. Then make up a folder for keeping *all* previous tax returns and store in the space you have chosen for items you will *never* throw out. Place it in your copy of last year's income tax return.

At the new year's beginning retire the folders of the current year. They now become records of *Former Years*. Some of them will be papers that must be kept always, and others can be discarded after a time. They should be stored in a safe, dry place, close by, if possible. (Just how long to keep various documents will be discussed later on in this chapter.)

The *Vital Papers* category consists of the items that are extremely difficult to replace, if indeed it is possible at all. These should go in a bank safe deposit box. In some states, safe deposit boxes are sealed when a box owner dies. To avoid this difficulty, some couples maintain two boxes. The box (or boxes) should not be used as a catch-all for souvenirs. Check out what insurance against theft the bank carries, and if your homeowner's insurance policy covers the contents of the box.

The *Urgent* category contains items that could be needed at any hour of the day or night, as, for example, insurance policies (life, auto, property) and passports. Many people keep these items in a safe deposit box. This can cause unnecessary delays such as in the case of an accident to a close family member in Europe, or elsewhere, when you must leave immediately. These are the items that are better kept near at hand, possibly in a small, portable strongbox.

The reason for a *portable* box is twofold. In the case of fire it is always extremely difficult to think of what to save. People have been known to rush out of a burning building with a Paris hat, or a saltshaker, and only afterwards wish they had managed to be more practical. Secondly, moving to a new home can be most disruptive to a record-keeping system. It is convenient, therefore, to have urgent papers in a portable condition.

The key to the safe deposit box is of special importance. It is probably the most difficult item of all to replace. The portable strongbox is a good place for it. Remember to make a card for it in the index box. You may not always be around to say where things are kept. The combination for any home safe can go in the strongbox, but cleverly concealed.

People have curious ways of hiding items of importance to conceal them from thieves or prying eyes. They put them in teapots, under mattresses, behind pictures, on top shelves of dark closets, and later on forget what went where. Even if this practice is followed, at least make a card for the index box to aid your memory.

Some people prefer to keep their wills and trusts in the office of an attorney or trust company for privacy. For more than privacy, these are the proper places for wills and trusts. But if you want to refer to them, this can be inconvenient. It is, therefore, handy to keep copies in the strongbox.

The category we have called *Valuables* can also be described as "personal" capital assets. This category includes all kinds of collections: guns, coins, stamps, first editions, works of fine art, to name a few. Antiques and jewelry belong here, though the latter is often stored in a bank vault. All these items should be regularly appraised and covered by insurance, and photographed, if possible. There should be an inventory, with one copy in the safe deposit box, and another with your insurance agent. The inventory should be updated every few years.

Many women experience terrible panic when they lose important papers or valuables. A card index box can solve the problem. For each vital and urgent item, there should be an index card stating where the item is located. Memory is not enough: make a card. Anything that is out of sight and put away should have a card. Build it up constantly. Put on a card a list of important contacts such as: tax counsel, attorney, banker, broker, insurance representatives, employer, mortgage holder. Women's lives are often divided into many roles, and they handle so many areas of living that they need every aid they can get to promote efficiency.

Not only is it important to know where papers are located, but how long to keep them. Too many makes for clutter, too few makes for document poverty. Some people keep everything and end up with their car in the driveway, and the garage used as a storage room. Others are compulsive cleaners and err in the other direction. The answer lies somewhere in between.

Some of the reasons for keeping documents are to establish the value of a purchase, to prove assertions on tax returns, to demonstrate ownership of property, to prove dates of acquisitions, to establish contractual rights and liabilities, to record tax payments, or to assist in future financial planning. Other reasons are to furnish directions for care or operation of possessions, or to tell what to do if you are out of the picture. When it appears that keeping a paper can serve no useful purpose, it's a good time to get rid of it.

For many people, what to do about cherished mementos is the hardest decision. For example, an old passport may recall a special occasion, but only a current one is of use. A family portrait is a precious heritage, but a photo of a new wing on the house is good tax backup material. Old property insurance policies are waste paper once a renewal policy is issued and approved by you. Souvenir keeping is a personal decision and not a business one, and it's important to think about and care for these two matters separately.

There are some documents or papers that must be permanently retained. Among them are all tax returns of prior years. The reason for this is that the Internal Revenue Service does not keep tax returns forever, and there are often items in tax returns that may provide needed information years later. The tax law provides that when valuable property is sold the tax can often be determined on the basis of how long the property was held. (This rule is being reviewed by Congress.) This information can turn up on an old tax return. Other items to keep always are: life insurance policies, checkbooks, and records of important purchases such as stocks and bonds, real estate, valuables, capital improvements, interest in a partnership, pension plan assets, and the canceled checks that go with them. For tax reasons, it is necessary to know what actually was paid for important things, and when the purchases were made.

There are other items that may be disposed of after a time. A passport should be kept until a new one is issued. Insurance policies (except for life) should be kept until you have received the renewals and checked them over. Paid bills that do not record important purchases can be discarded after a year. Bank statements can go after seven years. Tax backup material and canceled checks that do not record important transactions must be kept for seven years and then may be discarded.

One of the best ways to get an overall view of what is involved in financial management is to get a copy of a net worth statement from your bank. This is the form you must fill out when you apply for a loan. By the time you have filled it out you will have a list of your assets and liabilities. You will know how much cash is in savings and checking accounts, what is the market value of your house and other real estate, and the value of your household furnishings. You will have the blue book value of your automobile(s), and the cash value of life insurance. You will have today's value of any stocks and bonds you own, a note of money owed to you, and a record of other assets. As well, you will have a list of installment debts, with the balance due, the balance due on any mortgages, credit cards and charge accounts and a record of any other debts.

Another way to gain information on the subject of maintaining records is to go over a blank tax return form and the schedules that go with it. We live in a tax-oriented society, and it is well to be prepared and know what the Internal Revenue Service requires.

An example of a person who was not prepared comes from a tax court case (*Herrick* v. *Comr., T. C.*). His unpreparedness cost him a negligence penalty.

> "Petitioner, on brief, recognizes that his deduction for $20,000 of expenses incurred abroad and in California over a 2-month period promoting Redi-Smoke cooker is tenuous. He admits that there are *no substantiating records, documentation, or receipts for these expenditures;* he has not attempted to reconstruct his records and places the blame on his secretary, "who somehow *misplaced the file.*" He states that "all that can be said is that the money was sure spent in going around the various places in Europe" and Cali-

fornia promoting the Redi-Smoke cooker. However, the law is well settled that no deduction, under Section 162 or 212, shall be allowed for any expenditure for travel or entertainment unless the taxpayer substantiates the following elements for each such expenditure: (1) amount, (2) time and place of travel and entertainment, (3) business purpose, and (4) the business relationship to taxpayer of persons entertained. Section 274(d); Section 1.274-5(b)(1) and 5(b)(2), Income Tax Regs. Petitioner has made no attempt to substantiate these expenditures except by his own uncorroborated testimony and Section 274(d) requires corroborating evidence. We hold that petitioner is not entitled to a travel expense deduction, for 1972, in excess of that amount allowed by respondent.

"The final issue for our decision is whether respondent correctly asserted a Section 6653(a) penalty. The penalty was imposed and properly assessed in the notice of deficiency and therefore the burden of proof is upon petitioner to show respondent's determination to be in error. Rule 142(a), Tax Court Rules of Practice and Procedure. Inasmuch as petitioner presented *no evidence* concerning the issue, and in fact admitted that *he did not even know* what some of the disallowed expenses related to, we have no choice but to uphold the negligence penalty under section 6653(a)."

The chief facts that come to light upon reading this tax court memo are that ignorance is no excuse; losing files costs money; and records are essential.

A special problem for women results when husbands keep their wives in a state of financial ignorance and do not even explain what has been done about wills, insurance, retirement benefits, savings bank accounts, and investments. Wives need to be enlightened. Some are afraid to ask for the sake of family peace. We consider this a course that directly endangers their security and that of their children. Family peace is important, but no woman should allow her future to be jeopardized by ignorance. If such women become widowed or divorced, or their husbands become disabled, financial catastrophe can be the result. It is extremely important to know where documents are, who handles them, and what will be done in the event of any of the emergencies mentioned.

Getting the information may require tact and ingenuity. Each woman in this situation must judge for herself what steps to take. She can consider asking him outright, or requesting a conference with his lawyer or accountant. If she signs a joint return she is entitled to a copy, and if she can obtain it in no other way, she can write to the local Internal Revenue Service office and obtain one. This will give her some valuable information, but she will, in addition, have to find out who his legal and financial advisers are and how to reach them, where insurance policies are located, where his will is kept and what are the contents of his safe deposit box.

Another problem area lies in living together without formal marriage. The desire to avoid the hassles of marriage should not blind a woman to possible future pitfalls. For example, if she should pay for a share in the purchase of a vacation home, she should do so by check and clip that to her copy of the records of the transaction. These papers should go into her own safe deposit box. She should have a record of anything that she owns, be it furniture, property, jewelry, cars—everything. It is important to have records and to make provision for the disposal of such property in the event of separation or death, and the resultant claims of family and even friends. In some states, cohabitation may be recognized as a valid marriage after a period of time. In this event, particularly in a community property state, it is important to know what assets each of the partners brought into the relationship or inherited while they lived together.

When there are two wage-earners in the same family, financial independence should be maintained. Ideally, each spouse should have a checking and savings account. In addition, a joint account should be maintained for ordinary living expenses. When funds are kept separately a woman must, if possible, pay for some capital assets (a house, a car, important furniture purchases, etc.) and document her share in the acquisitions. She should keep canceled checks and other records of these transactions in her own safe deposit box. This is for estate tax reasons (see chapter 9, "Inheriting It").

In summary, planning is the key to efficient record-keeping and record-keeping is the key to efficient planning. It may seem difficult to anticipate the changes of a lifetime but good planning will allow for change and the simple records needed. Most women have at least four stages in their lives. There are the first of all the early years of education and preparation, then the beginning of a career, which may be marriage, salaried job, or both. Then comes the active phase of earning a living, developing a marriage partnership, raising children, or all three. Finally, comes the period that few women anticipate, and which may last for at least twenty years: widowhood, or retirement, or both. These can be her most productive years or her most barren. Financial independence for this time is built on the records of the previous years. No matter what her age or circumstances now, a woman must take charge of her financial life. We feel strongly that it's a mistake to live in helplessness or ignorance at any period. Take the first best steps—keep records and understand the documents you deal with—the sooner the better.

2

Earning It

The best way to earn money is to have the right job. It is all important to discover your talents and aptitudes and then match them up with job opportunities. This is true even if you have never worked and want to start late in life, or if you have always worked and want to change careers. Changing careers may mean being unemployed for several months and borrowing or invading a savings account to pay the entry into the new career.

As an example, a shop steward of a wire manufacturing company learned about his talents the hard way. One day he dropped a monkey wrench into a new $300,000 piece of equipment and was promptly fired for negligence. Before all this happened he served as chief union organizer for the company and had been negotiating wage demands with the company.

His union suspected he had been fired for his union activities and not for dropping the monkey wrench and complained to the National Labor Relations Board. The matter was resolved before a board of arbitration. The chief arbitrator said the man was an excellent union organizer and suggested he take some aptitude tests to find out what other job he could do. The tests showed that the man was clumsy but he had sales ability. Shortly thereafter he was given a job in the sales department. Not too many years later he was president of the company.

Aptitude testing can be a first important step in finding a job. A student can usually find testing at school. Any number of organizations give such tests, such as vocational and career guidance organizations, educational consultants and counselors, personnel consultants, business schools, or psychology departments of state universities. They are surprisingly reasonable in cost and often are free of charge. Financially speaking, never can so small an investment produce so large a return.

Aptitude testing gives guidelines about abilities: it does not find jobs. Jobs come through friends, relatives, former employers, employment agencies, or newspapers, the most obvious source being through employment agencies. The agency you choose is important. Try to find one that specializes in the type of job that interests you; or go directly to the personnel department of a firm that you would like to work for. Ask them which agency they use. Go to that agency and ask for the names of companies in that field.

Now you are ready to do some research. Visit your local library and look for articles in the periodical department about some of the companies whose names you have. Large companies are often written up in such magazines as *Fortune, Forbes, Business Week,* or *Dun's Review.* It should be a matter of most careful investigation to find the best companies in a chosen field. The choice of a job is too often left to chance. When you start a job on an impulse, you sometimes later learn that you could have worked in the same field for a far better company.

Other sources of information about companies are

friends and former schoolmates who may be in that field. If the stock of a company is publically traded, a stockbroker is a good source of information. Whether the job is in a major industry or in a small business, women need to check out the financial and other aspects of employment. In these days of galloping inflation it is of prime concern to chase the fugitive dollar with all the skill at your command.

When you have done your homework about the employment that interests you, then go to the employment agency you have selected armed with the following questions to consider before accepting any job offer:

What is the attitude toward woman workers?

Is there equal pay for men and women in the same job?

What are the fringe benefits? (Group health, cheap group life insurance, free parking, cheap company cafeteria, health and exercise facilities, merchandise at a discount, bonuses, pension and profit-sharing plans—see chapter 10, "Retiring on It")

Is there a cost-of-living adjustment built into the payroll policy?

Is the job unionized? (If there is a union shop, what is the tab to join?)

What kind of a reputation has the company in its field?

Has the company a reputation for fairness to employees?

Is there possibility for advancement?

What are the location and surroundings?

What are the job conditions? (Salary, vacation, hours, sick days, overtime)

Some women might look favorably on a change to another part of the country. It is important to know where the industry in question is advancing most rapidly. Try to find out where foreign investors are putting their money. If an area is attractive to foreign investors, it should be so for the native born as well. The Department of Commerce can answer this and other questions. Also query your stockbroker and banker. Even if, for personal reasons, you decide to go to a depressed area, at last you should know what you are getting into.

A beautician we knew wanted to open a beauty salon in another part of the country. She knew an executive in Clairol and asked him where Clairol was selling at the most rapidly increasing rate. When she found out, she moved to the area and has been very successful.

Another measuring device to use is to ask the Department of Commerce about the rate of employment and unemployment of women in a selected area. Find out where the rate is most favorable, and check the male unemployment. This will tell you if an area discriminates against women. Research will help you find the best place for relocation.

Fringe benefits are the easiest way to add tax-free dollars to your paycheck. When you realize the erosion to your income because of inflation and taxes, you must come to the conclusion that somehow you have got to get more spendable money into your pocketbook. Fringe benefits include retirement plans, profit-sharing plans, health insurance, bonuses, and vacation pay. Companies have booklets about these matters. Obtain a copy of the company booklet and read it. You will get valuable information. Most important is to be sure that the benefits will travel, that is to say, will go with you if you are fired or change jobs. This is known as "vesting." More often than not your nonvested interest is lost when you change jobs, usually retirement benefits.

For some jobs you have to sign an employment contract. If you do so, be sure they insert an "arbitration clause." This is the cheapest and quickest way to settle a dispute, should one arise. An example of an arbitration clause reads like this:

"Any disputes arising out of this Agreement shall be determined by arbitration in New York. The arbitrator shall have the power to provide intermediate relief and equitable relief as well as damages. This Arbitration Agreement shall survive the termination in other respects of this Agreement or any extension or amendment thereof. The arbitrator shall be entitled to award counsel fee or other expenses of arbitration as justice requires. A judgment or decree may be entered on such award in any court of competent jurisdiction. The Rules of the American Arbitration Association shall govern. This Agreement shall be binding on any successor or commonly controlled affiliate of either party."

What about equal pay for equal work? If a job pays a woman less than that received by men for comparable work, she should complain to the United States Equal Employment Opportunity Commission at the state or federal level, or her chapter of the National Organization of Women. You can find the United States Equal Employment Opportunity Commission located in Washington D.C. You can call them. Equalization will not be accomplished overnight.

Insurance benefits will also be written up in the fringe benefit booklet but it is hard for the layperson to evaluate them, and even the average insurance salesperson is unskilled in this subject. There are top-notch insurance people equipped for such an evaluation and a good place to get a recommendation for one is in the nearest law or business school.

The insurance benefits that should be checked out are not only the life insurance benefits, but also health and disability. The subject of life insurance, on one hand, and health, accident, and disability insurance, on the other hand, are fully discussed in later chapters. Usually an insurance agent will be glad to visit with you at your home and review the fringe benefit booklets of your employer or prospective employer and explain what benefits you have and what benefits, if any, are missing. We will discuss the method of evaluating and locating a good independent insurance agent in the subsequent chapters devoted to that subject. The subject is complicated, and in the field of disability benefits alone there are a bewildering variety of options (see chapter 7, "Insuring It").

If there is a union ask a union official about the status of the industry, and the company. Find out about union benefits. Remember that the union exists to protect your job and to prevent people from taking advantage of you. Is there a union shop you have to join and how much does it costs to join?

Nearly every job you take is covered by social security. More than nine out of every ten working people in the United States are building protection for themselves and their families under the social security system. The social security protection you earn stays with you when you change jobs; when you move from city to city; when you move to another state.

Certain things about social security are particularly important to women. Take, for example, the woman who works in a job or profession throughout her adult life. She is covered under social security while she works, and she's earning credit toward a monthly income for her retirement. If she's married and has children, she's also earning social security protection for her family—protection over and above what they already have, based on her husband's work. Even if a woman is single and has no dependents, the social security credits she earns count toward *monthly benefits for the family she may have in the future*.

To get any social security benefits you need credit for a certain amount of time spent in covered work. The amount of credit generally depends on your age when you become disabled, die, or retire. But if you stop working before you earn enough social security credits, *no benefits will be payable*. However, credits you have already earned remain on your work record, and you can always go back to work and earn any additional credits you need to get benefits. This is of great significance to the woman who decides to stay home while she raises children. When they are grown she can go back to work and earn additional necessary credits. Ten years of full time work will insure her fully for life. Generally, two years will give a minimum amount.

You can check your social security record, free of charge, by making a request for a statement of your earnings. Under present regulations you will not be told how much your benefits will be, but you will be told the amount of your social security earnings to date.

You may obtain a card for making this request from your nearest social security office. This you will find by looking in your telephone directory under "U.S. Government, Health, Education, and Welfare Department, Social Security Administration." In smaller towns that do not have an office, the yellow pages under "U.S. Government" will indicate the nearest office. The address for Social Security Headquarters is:

Social Security Administration
P. O. Box 57
Baltimore, Maryland 21203

You need a social security card if your work is covered by the social security law. Show your card to your employer when you start work or when you change jobs so that your wages will be properly credited to your earnings record. Your social security number is also used for income tax purposes. You may be asked to give your social security number to anyone who pays you dividends, interest, or other income that must be reported to the Internal Revenue Service. If you do not already have a social security number you can get an application for one from any social security office. You need only one number for your lifetime. If you change your name or if you lose your card, any social security representative will help you get a card showing your new name, or a duplicate of the card you lost. Whatever name you use in your employment should be on your card. Many women, for example, continue to work under their maiden names after they are married. This is the name that should be on the card. It is also allowable to work under your married name, provided you notify the social security administration of the change and get a new card. But the number will remain the same.

A particularly important point for women is that a wife who has earned her own social security credits has certain options at retirement. For example, suppose your husband continues to work past sixty-five and earns too much to get benefits. Or, suppose he is younger than you. *You can go ahead and retire on your own record.* Then when your husband actually retires, you can take the wife's payments if they are higher than yours. At age sixty-five, a woman gets the full wife's benefit which is fifty percent of the amount of her husband's benefit.

Social security is equally important to the wife who chooses the unsalaried work as homemaker. She's covered under social security through her husband's earnings and should know about the benefits she can get if he retires, becomes disabled, or dies. If he dies before retirement age, or is disabled, and she has children who are under eighteen, she can get benefits to help support them until they reach age eighteen. If they are full-time students in school, benefits are payable until they reach age twenty-two. When the children are no longer covered she will have no benefits, until she reaches age sixty, for widow's benefits or age sixty-two, for disability benefits.

If you are a divorced wife, you can get benefits when your ex-husband starts collecting retirement or disability payments at age sixty-two, provided you were married to him for ten years (prior to January 1, 1979, the required time was twenty years). You can also get payments if your ex-husband dies, if you are sixty or older (fifty if you are disabled), or if you have young children entitled to benefits on his record.

Effective January 1979, the widow who remarries at age sixty or older can continue to collect the widow's benefits of her deceased husband without any reduction in the amount. Ordinarily, a widow loses her social security rights when she remarries. After age sixty, according to the new regulations effective January 1979, a woman can take whichever is higher, either the benefits of her deceased husband or the wife's benefits of the new husband.

We cannot emphasize strongly enough the importance of social security coverage. An employer is breaking the law if he does not comply with social security regulations. It is the responsibility of the employer to see that wages paid are properly reported.

While you work, you also earn credits toward Medicare protection for yourself and your family. If you are eligible for a social security or railroad retirement check, either as a worker, dependent, or survivor, you also are entitled to Medicare insurance when you are sixty-five. It is a good idea to apply for your Medicare insurance three months before your birthday month. That way your protection will start the month you reach sixty-five. You *must* apply for Medicare, it does not start automatically. If you are still working at sixty-five, you can apply for Medicare, and pay a monthly premium for it until you retire.

One word of caution. Social security protection was never planned to provide a complete retirement income. It should be thought of as a supplement. It does not take away the need to build into your lifetime financial planning other forms of saving and investing. Even if you decide to be self-employed, you can build up social security credits. Your contribution will be a little over two thirds of the combined employee-employer rate for retirement, survivors, and disability insurance. The Medicare insurance contribution rate is the same for employers, employees, and self-employed persons.

There is now a guarantee in the law that social

security payments will be inflationproof. Benefits are increased automatically to keep pace with changes in the cost of living. Your social security retirement check is based on your average earnings over a period of years. For example, a person retiring at age sixty-five between June 1978 and June 1979, with an average lifetime monthly wage of $485, can expect a monthly check of $380.70 with a spouse of the same age getting $190.40, making a total of $571.10. This is according to social security tables presently in use. Starting in 1979, a new method of figuring benefits will apply affecting all those who die or become disabled and some who reach sixty-two in that year. The new "wage indexing" system uses some of the old rules; but earnings are mathematically "indexed" to reflect changes in general wage levels over the years. Once wages are indexed, a formula, rather than the benefit table, sets the benefit amount. Persons older than sixty-two in 1979 use the old system. It is sufficiently complicated to figure out your benefits to warrant your taking a trip to the nearest social security office to obtain help from one of their representatives. The closer you are to retirement, the easier it will be.

The most basic issue in choosing a job is the personal situation of the applicant. Everything may check out favorably in regard to salary, fringe benefits, aptitude for the job, and opportunity for advancement. Yet, your life situation may stand in the way. The single woman without dependents or other involvements has the most freedom of choice. Yet the single working woman may at some time along the way contemplate marriage, or the housewife at some point may contemplate a salaried job. In either event the job will be influenced by the marital status.

For example, two married women were top scientists with Celanese. The Celanese Corporation decided to move its research laboratories from the New York City area to Louisville, Kentucky and wanted to keep

the two women. In each case Celanese made it possible
for their husbands to move. One of the men was an accountant and Celanese relocated him without loss of
status in the Louisville office of a major accounting
firm. The other husband already worked for Celanese
and was given substantial inducements to move to
Kentucky.

On the other hand, there are women who want to stay
where they are and husbands who want to move. An
example is a woman lawyer employed by a large New
York City law firm who had just been offered a
partnership. At the same time her husband was con-
templating a transfer to California. They moved to
California and she had to pass the California State Bar
Examination and start all over again.

Sometimes personal and family gains must be
weighed against financial losses. The move may mean a
reduced salary for one partner, and moving costs that
must be borne by the couple, plus loss of community
relationships. In some cases it may be decided that it
is both financially and personally foolish to move.

Fortunately for those involved, some careers are more
transportable than others. Women in secretarial work,
nursing, teaching, dental hygiene, or who are artists,
writers, domestic workers, or consultants, such as interior designers, can relocate fairly easily. Women who
choose to be lawyers, doctors, actresses, civil service
or union employees are more apt to encounter financial
and emotional problems by moving.

Women lawyers or doctors need to be licensed in the
state where they practice their professions. This
frequently involves difficult examinations given by the
states because often the local attorneys and doctors
in operation do not take kindly to added competition
from people (particularly from women) moving into
their state.

The husband has the job all set up before he moves
if he makes a change within his own company. If he
wants to move to another location because it has more

job opportunities, it may turn out that while he is improving his business opportunities, his wife is losing out on hers.

Established actresses in cities such as New York or Los Angeles, for instance, will find it difficult to combine family life with a career if the husband moves to an area where there are either no theatres or only theatres which operate occasionally or during the summer.

Civil service employees may find that they lose rank, seniority, and may even have tó take a whole battery of tests in their field of civil service if their husbands want to move to another state, and sometimes even if they want to move from one city to another within the same state.

A union employee may discover that in her line of work there is either a different union or no union at all in the new location and may lose pension benefits as well as seniority in the move.

Besides finding out about aptitudes and talents, jobs and employers, the effects of marriage on a career, or moving from state to state, there is the equally important matter of long-term planning for a career. Men do the long-term goal-oriented planning better because traditionally they have had the historical role as providers, protectors, and supporters of families. Women, in contrast, have traditionally been looked after and have played a dependent role throughout the centuries. As men in school were zeroing in on the money-earning jobs, their sisters were thinking about life styles and personal fulfilment.

For example, we knew a talented young artist just out of college who decided to teach art while she was building up her artistic career, but she had neglected to take courses in education and could not qualify for the teaching job she sought. Instead she took a free course in computer programming and then earned her living for several years in this way. Then she married, had a child, and for many years combined art, part-time jobs, and marriage. It was not until she was in her forties that she finally became established as an artist and began selling her work. Had she given attention to financial goals, she could have become financially independent at a much earlier age. Accordingly, our advice to career-minded women is to take courses in college or elsewhere that will permit them to enter their chosen fields as professionals.

Not every woman chooses to go to college. For those who do not there are excellent alternatives. It is extremely useful to take an extensive and top-notch secretarial course. A secretary is on guard at the pearly gates of business progress. One of the most successful woman lawyers in New York City started as a secretary in a law office and then studied law at night. Secretarial work is not only a good standby, but can be a stepping stone up the financial ladder.

Real estate does not require a college degree and is a good field for women. It is compatible with marriage and is excellent training for investing in real estate. Many times an older woman or a widow will discover that her best possible investment is real estate. Already trained as a real estate salesperson or broker, she will be ahead of the game in handling her own financial matters.

Other types of skills which can be learned in youth and kept in reserve if the woman marries and decides to be a homemaker until the children are old enough to permit her to go to work, and which are also generally quite portable, are computer programming, selling (particularly in department stores or house-to-house canvassing such as Avon), some of the arts (but it may be difficult if your home is not located in the near vicinity of art galleries), restaurant work, motel and hotel management, travel, agenting, or cooking. If the latter is one of your goals, check with The Culinary Institute of America, P. O. Box 53, Hyde Park, N. Y. 12538, which runs a two-year course year round and claims that a graduating student gets at least three job offers. Cornell University in Ithaca, New York has a top reputation in training for hotel management.

Another highly portable job is that of a registered nurse, dental technician, or X-ray technician.

A course of study which can be invaluable is accounting. Not only will this help keep one's own financial and tax situation in line, but can help her husband, and she can find a good job anywhere she might want or need to move. States usually have less stringent regulation for accountants moving in than for lawyers or doctors.

Four of the best accountants we know are women (and there must be many hundreds more). One of these women has built up a notably successful career in a city of some 250,000 inhabitants in New England, another in a suburban community in New Jersey, a third in New York City, where the competition is fierce. The fourth started in Seattle, and when she and her husband decided to move to a farming community in eastern Washington State, it took her only a few months to reestablish a brand-new flourishing practice.

About fifty percent of the labor force in the country today is composed of women, and more than half of all adult women are now working or looking for work. Despite television commercials which depict women as a consumer class intent on taking out stains, pinching bread and toilet tissue, in actual fact they are not passive stay-at-homes, but are major participants in the American economy.

They now share with men the concerns of earning money. They are taxpayers, heads of households, in top management, in banking and publishing, and running their own businesses. (Practically every sizable corporation in the country is eagerly seeking women to qualify for top managerial posts. This is one of the areas where the Equal Employment Opportunity

Commission has most actively been checking for instances of discrimination.)

The success of women in establishing their own businesses has been phenomenal. One Connecticut woman started selling from her own home a new type of stove which would be placed in suburban fireplaces to provide household heat more efficiently. In her first year of business, she earned $23,000, and when a change of her husband's job location was to Florida she was able to sell the business to another woman at a good price.

More and more women are opening retail shops, especially in suburban communities. While some have failed, others have been highly successful. If you plan to do this, talk to the nearest U. S. Small Business Administration, to the most imaginative bank in the neighborhood, and get the best accountant and attorney available (we later write on the subject of selecting expert financial counselors).

It is essential that any capital of her own that a woman puts into opening a business, or any borrowed capital that is used in this fashion be employed in a manner where the frequent start-up losses will be deductible from ordinary income. This is discussed in detail in the chapter "Lending It."

Remember, if you are living in a community property state (described in chapter 13) one half of the business and one half of the income you create will belong to your husband. As soon as the new business "rounds the corner" financially and starts operating at a profit it will be well for the woman to consider having trusts for her children, either as partners in a family partnership or as stockholders in a corporation. This will reduce the income tax and estate or gift taxes and could help finance the college education of your children (see chapter 9, "Inheriting It"). It should be kept in mind, however, that a Subchapter S corporation, discussed in chapter 5, is usually disqualified if any of its stock is held by a trust. Since this qualification may be important while you are taking start-up losses, the use of trusts as stockholders or partners should be initiated as soon as possible after the enterprise starts breaking even.

Family partnerships between husband and wife provide wonderful outlets for a woman's energy and intelligence and frequently substantially increase the family income. By a decision in the federal court in South Dakota, one Besse Craig saved over $30,000 in estate taxes on the estate of her husband, Clarence, because the court found that Besse and Clarence had become partners in the farming business, with Besse supplying some of the capital, doing the bookkeeping, feeding the farmhands, and doing a lot of other chores such as assisting in the purchase of cattle at sales. However, the court ruling was achieved only after lengthy and expensive litigation because Besse and Clarence did not have a written partnership agreement. Had they consulted an expert in the field of taxation, all of this litigation could have been avoided through a relatively simple partnership agreement. The ground rules for a family partnership are laid down quite explicitly in Section 704(e) of the Internal Revenue Code and the Regulations thereunder. Your attorney or accountant should review these with you, and every year when you file a partnership return, you should recheck with your accountant and attorney to make sure you are sticking by the rules.

You should also check with your professional advisers on technical requirements of starting up a new business. You will need an Employer's Identification number, which your accountant or lawyer can obtain for you. If the enterprise is a limited partnership (where limited partners cannot be held responsible for partnership debts in excess of their original investment), the partnership agreement has to be filed and, in some states, advertised. In some states, the filing has to be in the county seat, in others, with the Clerk (or similar official) of the town where the partnership functions.

If you are qualified as a Subchapter S corporation, special forms have to be filed with the Internal Revenue Service by both the corporation and each and every stockholder. Moreover, a new stockholder coming in will have to file a form acquiescing in the Subchapter S corporation status. (Remember, these corporations are described in chapter 5.)

A corporation certificate must be obtained from the state in which the corporation is organized. Sometimes the name selected for a corporation is so similar to a corporation already in existence that you will be denied the use of the name. The availability of a corporate name should be checked before you invest too much time and money in popularizing the name. This can be done by your attorney.

Frequently an attorney or accountant will recommend that a corporation be incorporated under the laws of another state where the law is more liberal. Delaware and Nevada are among the popular states. But if you do this, you must "qualify" in any state where the corporation maintains a regular office. If this is not done, any contract made in such state will probably not be enforceable. Most women automatically incorporate in the state in which they live, but it is important to check with your accountant and attorney to see whether it would be better to incorporate in another state and then "qualify" in your home state.

If you do business as an individual, not under your own name, but under an assumed name, such as "Aunt Nellie's Restaurant," it is necessary in practically all states to file a certificate of doing business under an assumed name. In some states such certificates must be filed with the clerk of the town in which you operate and in others at the county seat.

It is of the greatest importance that you get financial, accounting, and legal advice before you start operating a business either from your home or outside it.

Women are enriching the economy with their talents and brain power. The move to financial independence by women has only just started, though it will be some time before new patterns of family and community life emerge and stabilize and become fully supportive of the woman money earner.

3

Spending It

Whatever you have is never enough. Living on credit, in debt, dreading April 15, trying to find money for a vacation, gifts, new car, while trying to stay abreast of the grocery bills—this is today's nightmare, a game of tag, with inflation chasing the paycheck. There are only two ways to go, either stretch the paycheck or trim the budget.

The most usual first choice is to trim the budget. This involves an eyeball to eyeball confrontation with the most pervasive and powerful force in our society— the advertising commercial, now generally referred to as a "message." The message is to keep up with your neighbors, be beautiful and comfortable, and in a nut-shell, buy utopia with your credit card. It is hard to resist.

Here is where financial planning comes in to direct traffic and route your income to superhighways instead of into dead-end streets. Before you spend the first dime, have a plan. The plan will list all the calls on your income in the order of importance. No matter how you twist or turn, probably the first call on your income had better be taxes. If you are self-employed, you will pay quarterly estimated taxes, the amount of each payment being based either on what you expect to make this year or on what you made last year. It is better to overestimate than to underestimate. At least, if you are over, you will get a refund, and that is always a pleasure. Since you know that you will have to make the payment every three months, it is most foolhardy not to make a weekly deposit so that you will have the money to pay the tax when the time comes. You will need to consult with an accountant to find out how much you should estimate.

However, when you are employed by someone else, the tax gets taken out of your check before you ever get it. This is the case with your social security payment as well. Your employer and you share the cost, dividing if half and half. Each pays 6.05 percent of your gross paycheck (1978–1980). The amount you pay is based on your wage or salary.

Then comes your contribution to your employer's insurance and retirement programs if you are lucky enough to have such an employer. These will also be discussed in the insurance and retirement chapters. When you finally get that paycheck, you will realize that such withholding nowadays is fairly significant. Even if you are self-employed, social security payments must be made. Social security is more fully discussed in the preceding chapter.

In addition to taxes and payroll deductions, other "musts" are rent, mortgage payments, utilities, car payments, medical bills, interest on loans and credit cards. On the foundation of prompt payment of the "musts," you build your financial credibility. And build and maintain it you must, because once lost, it is hard to regain. The computer knows all, and your financial future is far too important to allow yourself to rest on a shaky financial foundation. Your credit history is a precious asset. Since the Equal Credit Opportunity

Act, women can now get credit in their own names, and married women have the right to their own credit history.

Should you ever lapse, there is one rule to follow and that is to pick up the telephone and call your creditor and explain your predicament. They know as well as you that nothing is easy. You will find them quite reasonable. What creditors cannot stand is if you seem to have disappeared. Often they will suggest ways for you to pay. But just let them know that you are really trying. Don't panic. Remember, there is always some arrangement that you can make. They look for your "ability and willingness to pay." When you have built up your financial reputation, then you will be eligible to get credit cards and other forms of credit to make your spending more convenient and to give you financial protection in emergencies. In addition, credit cards provide a form of identification in a way nothing else will.

When you have a credit card, you should be aware that you have started a relationship with a computer. When you want to rectify an overpayment, or you have some other problem with your billing, it is useless to get angry—the computer has no understanding of emotions. The way to get its attention is to tear the billing card or statement in half and return it together with a letter explaining the situation. Address the letter to a specific person such as the president of the corporation, or the head of the credit department. Otherwise, you will be passed from person to person and suffer endless and exasperating delays. If you want to phone, call collect. If nothing works, send copies of your correspondence to the Better Business Bureau, the President's Commission on Consumer Affairs, your state attorney general, or your local consumer help office.

The next item on your list after the "musts" is "necessities." Here you can use a great deal of picking and choosing. Picture to yourself two grocery carts.

One is filled with wine, cartons of cigarettes, soft drinks, steak, cookies, cakes, pies, paper products, and even bird seed. The other cart is filled with items of solid food value, calculated to produce in you the maximum of bone, muscle, and energy. It is not our purpose to suggest the choices you should make but merely to point out that the result should be a balance between instant enjoyment and future security.

Do what you will, it does often come down to a situation where you find yourself carrying a constant debt load. When this happens to a married couple, the answer often is to introduce a second paycheck into the home. The husband may choose to moonlight, or the wife may take a job. Even for unmarried individuals, the choice is much the same, though a single person will often opt for changing to a better job, a choice that is not quite so easy for a married person. A better job will make it unnecessary to trim the budget drastically.

In any event, when you know what income is available, it comes down to cutting it up like a pie into the sections we have mentioned above. To summarize:

1. Musts—taxes, payroll deductions, rent, mortgage utilities, automobile, loan interest, credit cards
2. Necessities—food, clothing, amenities of living, basic saving and basic insurance.
3. Discretionary Funds—Luxury spending —Saving or investing or insurance

There is great flexibility in all three categories, and opportunities to change the type of pie and the number of slices. Maybe a Boston cream pie is too rich, and you can make do with a plain old apple pie. Maybe the pie is too small and your low-yield job won't buy you a bigger pie. Try to upgrade yourself with more education and a better-paying job. Maybe your financial record-keeping is in a shambles and you are not keeping records of what you are spending. Sharpen your pencil and make a better diagram for cutting up your income pie. If you have debts, make sure that the carrying charges on them total no more than 10 percent of your annual income. If they are more, allow yourself no more luxury spending until your debt is reduced. You will find that you will have to revise your plan from time to time to fit the changing patterns of your life.

As a debtor you should know that you have some rights. For example, the House Banking Committee has approved legislation to protect consumers from harassment and unethical practices by debt collectors. The bill provides criminal penalties for use of abusive or obscene language by debt collectors in telephone conversations, phony documents or court materials sent by mail, harassing phone calls to a debtor's place of employment or neighbors or relatives, and any misrepresentation of the collector's true identity. To prevent collectors from harassing the wrong person, the bill requires collectors upon request to validate in writing that the person actually owes the debt.

When you have amassed sufficient discretionary funds to consider building your own house, you decide, let us say, to buy a perfectly beautiful suburban building lot that is also a piece of unimproved real estate. Here is a real case of "buyer beware." What many Americans do not realize is that they will be faced with ever-lengthening delays in getting approval to build. At the present time local conservation commissions can delay permission for months and often years. Should there be "wetlands" on the property the final authority is the Army Corps of Engineers. Planning and zoning commissions are equally slow in approval granting. The individual buyer can be badly held up through his own unfamiliarity with the necessary procedures. "The Goodkin Report," a monthly newsletter of the home construction industry, estimates that on a modest

$30,000 home, delays can add up to over $5,000 a year to the cost. This includes land-holding costs for unimproved property, interest, taxes, insurance, and inflation costs associated with escalating construction costs. The best bet for the prospective home builder is to look for an "approved" building lot. This will cost more initially, but the cost will include a certified survey, a topographical map, and locations drawn in and approved for driveways, homesite, and well. All Mr. and Mrs. Home Builder have to do is go ahead and build.

The present overlapping, duplicative, inconsistent, and uncoordinated regulations are totally out of control, and it is to be hoped that soon all existing regulations will be rigorously coordinated so that the business of granting approvals can be speeded up. In view of the possible problems, we strongly recommend that if you buy unimproved land, you employ a lawyer skilled in real estate and knowledgeable about local boards and commissions. In the end it will save you money.

Some home-seekers have become so discouraged by the delays and rising costs of building that they turn instead to purchasing an existing house. There are less headaches all round. But before you buy, look into what are called the "contingencies." These are the mortgage arrangements, building inspection, termite inspection, and well inspection. These costs must be borne by the buyer, unless otherwise arranged. In this case, also, it is well to have a knowledgeable lawyer to pilot you through the maze.

However, if despite the difficulties you decide to build your own house, it is important that you have a carefully drawn contract with your builder to protect you from delay and financial irresponsibility. In some cases it happens that a builder is so busy that he drags out completion interminably while working on other jobs, or he may be so underfinanced that he goes broke. Protection can be obtained against these things in a contract that should contain the following:

1. A provision that the contractor is paid in installments and that all payments have a portion reserved to secure the faithful completion of the contract. The reserve fund should be payable on completion of the job subject to an inspection for errors and omissions.

2. A completion date with a penalty clause in increasing amounts if the date is not met.

3. A completion bond guaranteeing the faithful fulfilment of the contract. If the contractor quits or goes broke when the building is half-completed, not only will there be extensive costs for the delay involved in getting another contractor, but the cost of completion will eventually be far more than was contemplated. This can be protected against through a completion bond and a well-drawn contract. In view of the delays caused by litigation and the inevitable unforeseen situations that develop in any building contract, it is well to have an arbitration clause. Arbitration is speedier and less costly than litigation and is subject to the rules of the American Arbitration Association. Here is a good arbitration clause:

"Any disputes between the parties hereto arising from or involving this agreement are to be decided by arbitration in New York (or your state) pursuant to the rules of the American Arbitration Association, of which notice may be given by certified or registered mail to the last known address of all of the parties involved in such dispute. The arbiters shall be entitled to award counsel fee in their discretion and a judgment or decree (which may include equitable relief) may be entered in any court of competent jurisdiction on such award."

With regard to termite inspection, be sure to get competitive bids. And make careful inquiries about the reputation of the firm you call in. There are reputable firms, but also, unfortunately, there are those who prey on the homeowner or purchaser by charging four or five times what the job is worth.

The best safeguards against all swindles are as follows:

1. Be on guard when you are in an emotional state.
2. Deal with well-established companies.
3. Insist on a clear contract and check it with an attorney if any substantial amount is involved.
4. Check with the Better Business Bureau.
5. Get a bank reference.
6. Make a price comparison with identical products.
7. Do not sign a "negotiable" promissory note containing the words "pay to the order of." Such a note can be sold to a bank or finance company, and you end up being forced to pay because the bank or finance company are held harmless, even if the services were misrepresented.
8. Be sure your contract is signed by an officer of a well-known corporation. Don't take either oral or written representations of a salesperson.
9. If you can't afford a lawyer, get hold of the local Legal Aid Society or a neighborhood lawyer.

Another situation in which clear writing is necessary is in buying a car. Be sure all the warranties are in writing. Sometimes a salesperson may give you an oral warranty. You will be unable to prove additional oral warranties. When you are financing your car, compare the cost of financing through GMAC (General Motors Acceptance Corporation), for example, and your own bank. Frequently it is far more economical to finance through your bank. Go to the bank, tell them how much money you need, take the check to the car company, and buy the car outright from them. Your repayment will be a monthly amount to your bank. When you receive the car title, put it in your safe deposit box. This is one of the most easily mislaid documents, and you will need it when you sell your car.

Of greatest importance is the rule that when you are spending substantial amounts of your money and written contracts are involved, retain a copy of every single document you sign. This includes receipts, contracts, leases, construction agreements, purchase agreements, business letters. It is amazing how often a lawyer is precluded from giving effective advice to a client because documents are missing. Every woman should have two large signs on her desk, one saying "Get it in writing," and the other saying "Keep a copy."

This is the moment to talk about getting a good lawyer. Remember that every legal matter is unique. In drawing wills, for example, no two wills are remotely like each other. The same is true of contracts. Just because a law firm is large and impressive does not mean that you will receive the meticulous and particular attention your unique matter deserves. The reputation of the firm is not enough to ensure the competence of a particular lawyer who is handling your case. You must be particularly careful to make specific inquiries regarding experience in a given field.

The business of qualifying an attorney ahead of time is discussed in the last chapter in the book, "Selecting Your Professional Financial Advisers."

The soundest approach to the problem is to have a family lawyer on the same basis as you have, or should have, a family doctor, and make it your business to maintain contact on a regular schedule.

The time to change lawyers is not after a big mistake, but after a little one. When you buy a house, the lawyer should go over the contract. Every time you have a contract for work consisting of fifty dollars or more, it should be in writing. If you do no more than write it out yourself and read it over the phone to your lawyer, you are at least maintaining contact and ensuring your own safety. In most instances you can arrange with your family lawyer to be available for counseling for a relatively small amount on an annual standby basis. You can ask what kinds of situations you should check out. If your family lawyer proves competent in your regular work, then you will build up a history of experience and establish a feeling of confidence for the large matters.

It is a good idea to have an advance arrangement with your lawyer regarding fees. Never be afraid to discuss fees. It is your money. Try and find out if malpractice insurance is carried, just in case this should turn out very badly and you might have cause to sue.

Lawyers are sometimes paid on an hourly basis. Ask what the hourly charge is. Ask for a regular report regarding the status of charges to you, such as every month or three months. Sometimes there is a fixed fee for a particular piece of work, and this can be settled in advance. In this case, the time may be minuscule, but the years of experience and training will stand behind a simple yes or no. Sometimes lawyers work on a "contingent" basis, that is to say they will receive a percentage of what they recover for you, or save for you. If you are short of money, be fair to your lawyer and say so, and arrange to pay over a period of time. Even lawyers are sometimes willing to do this.

As mentioned in chapter 1, have a card for "Attorney" in your card index box. While it is all right to look for bargains in lawyers, occasionally it is better to pay a larger fee and get good results than to risk finding yourself in the hands of an incompetent lawyer and having to go to another lawyer to finish the job. The law in most states provides an absolute right to change lawyers with or without reason at any time. In any event, don't make your choice on the basis of fees alone. The most expensive gun you can get is the one that doesn't fire when you pull the trigger!

One of the finest legal developments today is the "Neighborhood Lawyer" setup. They are available to families with certain financial limitations. These lawyers are usually dedicated young lawyers, some of them brilliant, who are willing to work for community welfare at a relatively low salary.

When your feet itch to travel, there are many ways you can help to stretch your dollars. Naturally, a good travel agent can be a tremendous help, but you can also do it yourself if you are a really adventurous soul. You can also do a combination of both. Here are a few do-it-yourself ideas:

1. Read the travel sections of newspapers, especially over weekends.
2. Browse through the travel sections of bookstores and lending libraries. There are books for every possible kind of travel.
3. Keep a vacation file of clippings and pamphlets. You can get many interesting pamphlets from airline companies.
4. Use toll-free numbers to call airlines, hotels, credit car companies.
5. Become aware of off-season rates.
6. In the United States learn about land-air travel packages offered by airlines. You may have to spend a couple of nights in a less than exotic motel, but it's worth the savings in dollars.
7. Watch for newly developing areas where the prices have not reached the peak.
8. Watch for countries where the American dollar goes farthest, for example, Costa Rica and Canada.

9. Find out about rail passes in Europe. These must be purchased in the U. S. before you leave. There are the following: Germanrail Tourist Card, Scottish Travelpass, Britrailpass, French unlimited rail pass, the go-anywhere-anytime Austrian Ticket, the Italian rail ticket, and the Swiss Holiday card.

10. Look into inexpensive walking tours. Several European cities offer them. London has a great selection.

11. Try bicycling in Holland. It's as flat as a newly ironed sheet.

12. Look into tramp steamers. These are so popular that you must make arrangements about a year in advance.

13. Look into home exchanges. Ask a travel agent how you can swap home for a vacation.

14. Avoid renting or buying goods or services in airports. Except for duty-free shops, the prices are usually higher.

If your interest lies in further education, that is to say, postsecondary education ("postsecondary" means any formal education beyond the high school level), try supplementing your funds by means of scholarships, grants, or loans. Scholarships and grants are gifts and do not have to be repaid.* They are awarded on the basis of academic ability and financial need, or financial need alone.

Loans have to be repaid. If you have a loan, be sure you know when it has to be repaid, what the penalty for prerepayment is, what the carrying charges are.

You can find out about Basic Educational Opportunity Grants by writing to Basic Grants, P. O. Box 84, Washington, D. C. 20044. You can find out about National Direct Student Loans (NDSL) from the finan-

---

* They are tax free if the student is not required to do any special work such as research or writing, apart from the requirements for all students.

cial aid officer at the postsecondary school you would like to attend. From the same officer you can learn about the College Work-Study program, as well as the SEOG—a cash grant used to subsidize any student with a high need.

Arrange to take the Scholastic Aptitude Test (SAT) if you are applying for a scholarship that requires an SAT score. Application procedures vary from school to school. To find out how to apply, contact the financial aid officer or the office of the dean of students well before the term begins.

It's never too early to begin arranging for financial aid. It's a good idea to start at least a year in advance because some sources of aid process applications and make awards only once a year.

Other sources of aid for women include women's professional associations, foundations, service clubs and civic groups, and manufacturers of products for women. Various cities and some postsecondary schools have women's centers that provide information on financial aid and other career-related areas. Many scholarships, fellowships, grants, and loans are offered exclusively or with preference to minority students. To find these sources of aid, consult reference books in the library and check with your postsecondary school's financial aid officer.

State governments are another source of financial aid. For example, in California, there is the Student Aid Commission, which administers virtually all aid programs offered by California. You can write for information to the commission at 1410 Fifth Street, Sacramento, CA 95814. There are state scholarships, college opportunity grants, occupational education and training grants, and state graduate fellowships. Check your own state for opportunities.

You can save on education expenses in three ways— by cutting down on the time you spend in school, by choosing a less expensive school to attend, and by combining a paying job with your studies. One time-saver is to see if you can get extra credits through learning you have gained through jobs, travel, or volunteer work. To get credit, check with a professor in the field you plan to go into. You can also gain credits by taking tests conducted by the College Level Examination Program (CLEP). For more information, write to either CLEP, P.O. Box 1025, Berkeley, CA 94701; or to CLEP, P.O. Box 2815, Princeton, NJ 08540.

If you are a parent, devise a program for accumulating money for your child's postsecondary education as early as possible. Many experts say you should do this no later than your child's seventh birthday. Ideally, you should start saving within a few years of your child's birth. You may be able to use the cash of a whole life insurance policy as collateral to borrow from the insurance company if you have not been able earlier to accumulate funds. But remember that the policy's death benefit will be reduced until the loan is repaid. You can also check with the financial aid officer at your child's postsecondary school to find out whether the school offers loans to parents. Such loans generally involve interest rates lower than those of private lenders. You can also apply for loans for educational purposes at banks, savings and loan associations, credit unions, and other private lenders. Check chapter 9, "Inheriting It," for ideas of what grandparents can do.

Earlier in this chapter we spoke of using discretionary funds as a means to saving. There are three major forms of savings accounts:

1. Savings banks
2. Savings and loan associations
3. Savings accounts in commercial banks

A fourth is to save your money in a credit union of your place of employment. In all of these your savings are subject to withdrawal at will. In recent years it has become popular to make deposits for a fixed term such as ninety days, a year, three years, nine years, or the like. In such cases the deposit pays a rate of interest several points over that paid on demand accounts, where your deposit may be withdrawn at any time without penalty. The fixed-term deposit may also be withdrawn at any time, but with a stiff penalty.

The longer term deposits in early 1978 offered a doubling of your deposit if preserved intact for nine years (less the tax you have to pay on the interest).

The question is, What are you willing to sacrifice for total liquidity? The more immediately available your funds are the less the interest will be. But the lower interest rate does not always result in less ultimate money accumulation.

In the chapter dealing with real estate investments we tell the story of the investor who lost the chance for an ideal real estate investment because of the unavailability of a relatively small amount of cash. Because of investment opportunities such as this, which may come only once in a decade, it is our recommendation that you build up an emergency fund in a demand savings account so that when opportunity knocks at your door you are ready to move.

Such deposits, as stated, are available and necessary for all kinds of special needs in addition to their use for investments of special opportunity. (Even in such cases the savings account should be replenished as soon as possible.) Such accounts are needed in case of illness and accident costs not covered by insurance; also to meet the costs of unemployment.

There is some variety of interest paid on savings accounts, though the rate is governed by law. Savings and loan associations traditionally pay a little higher than savings banks, and both are a little higher than commercial banks. It pays to shop around. The institutions with lower allowable rates endeavor to overcome this differential by offering other advantages.

Savings accounts may be jointly held between husband and wife or mother and child. These have estate tax disadvantages when an estate (including insurance) exceeds $300,000. But for a moderate sum, these joint accounts can be very advantageous in providing immediate funds to the survivor in case of the death of one of the joint holders of the account. Moreover, no probate expenses and delay are involved in this situation. However, you should check whether or not local banks "freeze" (hold up withdrawal) from such accounts upon learning of the death of one of the depositors. New York is one such state, but Connecticut does not freeze accounts. Check the practice in your own locality.

One other source of emergency cash is the cash surrender value of a permanent life insurance policy. The nature and principles of such cash value will be more extensively discussed in the chapter dealing with insurance. At the moment, let us say that permanent insurance (as opposed to term) does produce cash values (usually after the first year, except in the case of a few policies which do have a small first-year cash value).

Unlike a savings account, a dollar of premium does not provide a dollar available for withdrawal. Of course, even savings deposits for a specified period of months or years cannot be withdrawn without a sacrifice of a portion of the higher interest rate offered on such accounts. Nevertheless, such deposits are available on a dollar-for-dollar basis, plus some interest.

The reason that the cash value of insurance policies usually (but not always) is not equal to premiums paid is that part of such premiums have been set aside for a mortality reserve (as later explained) and also are used to pay administrative expenses. However, the insurance features do have their function, and the availability of cash values as an emergency reserve should be kept in mind.

As will be pointed out in chapter 5, "Lending It," bonds, even government bonds, are frequently not salable at their face value (amount payable at maturity) and thus do not necessarily provide a source of readily available cash either for emergency or to meet unusually favorable investment opportunities.

Many, many highly profitable and valuable businesses have been built or bought by using a savings account for a down payment or initial investment. The balance of investment can usually be paid out from earnings or used to repay the loan which was employed either to acquire a going business or for the start-up costs of a new business. Thus, a savings account, balanced with essential insurance, provides an invaluable and necessary basis for financial security planning.

A good rule of thumb is that such an account should be built up to at least six months' living costs. Such costs need not include an allowance for medical expenses, except to the extent that they are not covered by your own, employer-supplied, or government-supplied health and surgical insurance. Whatever you save is a personal choice, just as the ability to postpone enjoyment is an individual matter; yet this process of investment is as old as civilization. Perhaps the oldest record of it is the story of Joseph of Egypt and his seven-year program of wheat storage against the seven years of famine—all as told in the Book of Genesis.

4

Investing It

When the time comes in your earning and spending experience that you are a little bit ahead, you may want to consider investing some surplus funds. Perhaps you have received a gift or an inheritance, the proceeds of life insurance, or you have sold something of value or have received the proceeds of a pension plan, a profit-sharing plan, or a stock bonus plan. Maybe you won a large sum in a lottery or have built up a sizable savings account from surplus income. These surplus funds are thought of as "capital dollars," and there is more you can do with them than putting them under the mattress. The capital dollars should be thought of differently from income dollars. Income dollars should buy your daily living, and capital dollars should buy your future security.

Before even thinking of investing, you should have an income, either earned or unearned, or both, sufficient to look after your basic needs and those of your dependents, if you have any. Then you will need a nest egg for emergencies, the size of which will vary depending on your overall financial picture. For some, two months of living expenses may seem princely, but for others the equivalent of one or two years' income may seem essential. In addition, you should have insurance protection to cover the eventualities of death, ill health, liability, and property loss or damage.

An investment program is safe to contemplate when you have nailed down a solid platform for daily living. It should be a balanced and comprehensive investment program; that is to say, only part of your funds should go into the stock market. By comprehensive, we mean not putting all your eggs in one basket. By balanced, we mean ranging from speculative to superconservative.

Investments in the stock market can be either highly speculative or superconservative. Contrary to what you might think, a woman with moderate funds is better off seeking the less conservative forms of stock market investment, carefully chosen, yes, but speculative, as contrasted with, say, the bond market. The goal of investing is to create capital, and the stock market is one means to this end. With capital it is possible to build more capital. Without it, the only means to success is to take a carefully calculated risk. In other words, you need to get into a growth situation to help you to avoid the inroads that inflation makes on your fixed income.

Inflation causes the purchasing power of the dollar to shrink and creates a need to invest part of your dollars in stocks that will grow in value and give you a hedge against inflation. A "hedge" means protection. We all know that the dollar of today does not buy what it used to buy five or ten years ago. This means that we need assets that are constantly growing in value, like, for instance, a piece of real estate that sold for $2,000 in 1958 and for over $60,000 in 1978. Lucky is the person who finds such a hedge! The person hardest hit by inflation is a widow or a retired couple on a fixed pension. Economize as she may, year by year her fixed dollar of income buys less and less. Unless she can get assets that grow in value she is at the mercy of inflation.

As you look at your overall financial picture preparatory to starting an investment program, you may find you are ahead of the game in your future security building. You may already have access to some financial security in the form of employer-supplied security like the fringe benefits of health insurance, participation in profit sharing or pension funds, Keogh plans (from an individual employer), group life insurance, "split dollar" life insurance, salary continuance plans, or disability insurance. Find out what your fringe benefits are. Ask your husband, if he is the breadwinner. It goes without saying that the person who has access to fringe benefits has a head start in planning for investing.

If you, or you and your husband are employed in work that offers no fringe benefits, you will have to provide your own platform of basic financial assets before you start your investment program. You will need reserves that you provide for yourself rather than get from your employer. A good starting point is a savings account into which you make regular payments. As well, you should have insurance on yourself, or on your husband, that will build up cash reserves (see chapter 7, "Insuring It"). It may also be possible for you to seek other employment with the advantages of employer-supplied security, as described in the preceding paragraph.

THE STOCK MARKET

Let us now assume that you are ready to invest, but you know little or nothing about stocks and bonds. You do not know what it means to be a stockholder. What it means is that you become a part owner in a business venture. You do this by investing in a company or corporation. Your money, and that of your fellow stockholders, provides the working capital for a particular corporation. The corporation depends on you, the public, for its financial needs. In return, they promise you a piece of the action when you purchase their securities, that is, their stocks and bonds.

As stockholder and also part owner, you are technically responsible for electing the directors of the company, though most stockholders generally empower someone else to do this for them by means of a proxy form that comes to you in the mail. It says something like "this form which you have signed will empower those of us who attend the meeting of stockholders to vote for you." The job of directors is to elect the officers of the corporation, who run it on a day-to-day basis. Some of the operations of the corporation require the approval of the board of directors, such as the decision to vote payment of dividends to the stockholders. Dividends are paid to the stockholders out of the surplus funds of the corporation after major business obligations are met. Dividends are your reward for investing in the business. If the business prospers, your dividends increase, and so does the value of each of your shares of stock. It is true that if the business does not prosper, you risk the loss of your investment, but bad as this is, you are not responsible for any of the debts of the corporation. You have no liability for the debts of the corporation.

Stockholders lose when business is bad and gain when it is good. Dividends are not always sure. They are paid only when the board of directors decides to pay them. However, if directors accumulate surplus beyond all reason, the courts can compel them to declare dividends. Sometimes a corporation may pay a dividend not in cash but in its own stock. The directors may announce that the stockholders will receive a certain number of shares of stock for every ten shares they own. Such stock dividends are usually not taxable. Some companies, such as International Business Machines (IBM), traditionally declare stock dividends. Cash dividends are taxable as ordinary income as a rule, but if the stock is sold at a profit, the profit is taxed as a capital gain and this can be at a lower rate than the tax on ordinary income. If the enterprise is successful, the value of your stock goes up. However, why the stock market goes up and down is a mysterious business, compounded of many factors. All that can be said at this juncture is that the value of stock tends to reflect the current business situation as well as the condition of your corporation. You will find generally that your dividend goes up in step with inflation if your corporation has also increased its earnings. A dividend that paid you, let us say, $280 last year, may well be paying you $294 this year.

There are different classes of stock. For example, some stock may be voting stock and some nonvoting stock. Frequently, a corporation which is very profitably operated and is closely held (managed by a family or small group) offers additional shares of stock to the public, but without voting rights. Because the public feels confidence in a supersuccessful corporation, the nonvoting stock will find a ready market. In actual fact, such a large proportion of holders of voting stock fail to vote at annual stockholders' meetings that a group that controls as little as 20 or 30 percent of the outstanding voting stock usually has what is known as "working control" of a corporation.

Corporations have other vehicles than stocks for obtaining capital funds for the development of their enterprise, among them bonds, debentures, convertible debentures, and convertible perferred stock. Bondholders occupy a very different position from that held by stockholders. A bondholder is a creditor of the corporation. The corporation acts here as a "borrower." In other words, the bondholder is lending the corporation money. The bond pays him interest. The bond has a maturity date when it will be repaid. Also, the bondholder's interests are represented by a trustee, usually a trust company. The corporation gives a mortgage on some or all of its property to the trustee as security for the payment of the bonds and the interest on the bonds. If there is a default, it is up to the trustee to foreclose the mortgage. These rights are controlled by what is known as a bond indenture.

Bonds that are not secured by a mortgage are called debentures. In that case, the debenture holders are still creditors but do not have a direct lien on a specific piece of property for their security. Debentures, therefore, have somewhat less security than bonds, but usually pay a somewhat higher rate of interest. The interest is normally a fixed obligation which must be paid regardless of whether or not the company is operating profitably. There are some exceptions. These are rare and are known as income bonds. On income bonds, the interest is payable only if earned (i.e. the corporation is operating at a profit). All interest is deductible in the same fashion as a business expense by the corporation in computing its net taxable income. The bondholders and debenture holders have no voice in the management of the business, except that their trustee can and must enforce the indenture under which the bonds or debentures are issued. The bondholders, for example, have nothing to say in such matters as who shall be the president of the company or whether or not the company should expand into new areas of activity.

Bonds or debentures can be traded, bought, and sold. If the corporation goes out of business, the bondholders and the debenture holders must be paid off first, before the stockholders get anything. The price of a bond depends on its safety, that is, the assurance the bondholder has that the interest will be paid, and that the principal will also be paid when due plus the interest rate it earns.

In recent years, a new type of security has developed. This is known as the convertible debenture. The holder of a convertible debenture (often known by stockbrokers as a convertible bond) has the advantageous position of a creditor but is also given the option to convert the debenture into common stock. For example, the holder of a $1,000 convertible may be given the privilege of surrendering the bond for fifty shares of common stock which, let us say, are selling at $17 a share. (50 × $17 = $850) This gives him only $850 for his $1,000 convertible. Following the principle of selling "dear," the time to convert the debenture would be when the stock was high. Let us suppose that the stock goes up in value from $17 to $22 a share. The debenture holder now can trade the convertible debenture into fifty shares of stock at a profit. (50 × $22 = $1100) The profit of $100 is treated as a capital gain over the debenture investment. Into the bargain there is no commission when you convert to common stock.

As you probably know, when you buy or sell stock, you do it through a broker who receives a commission on the transaction. But when you convert debentures into stock, the broker receives no commission but will be glad to perform the service if you are a good customer. If not, you may also make the switch to debentures through the transfer agent of the corporation.

Preferred convertibles are preferred shares which may be similarly converted into common stock. Many sophisticated investors feel that "convertibles" are the most favored form of stock market investment. They have the safety factor of debt securities, such as debentures, but they can also participate in the inflationary thrust of common stock. You may have to wait months to locate a good convertible selling at a reasonable premium. Going back to the example of the $1,000 debenture, if the stock is selling at $17 per share, and you are allowed to convert the debenture into fifty shares of stock, which come to $850 (50 × 17 = $850), the premium is $150 ($1,000 − $850 = $150).

In other words, you have paid $150 more for the debenture than the value of the stock you could convert it to. You can also buy at what is called "conversion parity." This would happen if the stock were selling at $20 a share, (50 × $20 = $1,000). In this instance, the face amount of the debenture of $1,000 is identical with the amount you could convert it into. Unless it is a very good issue with the prospect of going higher, you should not buy when the stock is selling below parity. Also, you must find a convertible in a corporation whose common stock has good growth potential and which is safe on the downside, meaning a company which can be relied on to pay interest and principal on the bond if business goes bad.

The wait is worthwhile. But don't invest heavily without an education in convertibles.

Perhaps here is a good place to mention the type of bond issued by a state or an agency of a state, such as a village, town, city, or some special state-owned organization such as the Port Authority of New York. Since the federal government is supposed to have no control over the states, except in certain narrow areas, it has been held by the courts that interest paid on these state or municipal bonds is exempt from federal income taxation. If a municipality issues bonds to pay for a special facility such as a new factory that it builds and leases for the purpose of creating new jobs, and the revenue you receive comes directly from this project, these are called "revenue bonds." But if the same state or municipality issues bonds of a general nature, secured by the general credit of a city or state, these are called "general credit bonds." Because of the wage and pension demands of state and municipality employees, the financial position of many states and cities has become weakened. Think of the situation of New York City, for example. For this reason, the "revenue bonds" are considered by some investors a good deal safer today than "general credit bonds."

There are five ways you can enter the stock market:

1. Join an investment club.
2. Employ an investment consultant.
3. Choose a stockbroker.
4. Invest in mutual funds.
5. Use a trust company.

The growth of investment clubs is one of the most interesting and encouraging phenomena of our current business scene. They are usually started by small groups of women or men. The members of investment clubs make regular investments as a group through the club, usually on a monthly basis. Generally the clubs meet once a month and hear reports from their members on one or several companies which are investment prospects. Occasionally, outside speakers are heard.

There is no substitute for direct experience in investing. After you or your fellow club members have studied various companies and have made small investments, and observed what happens: this is practical experience. If you want to join or form an investment club, you may obtain information from a well-established brokerage firm about area investment-club activity.

If not an investment club, you might start by investing in mutual funds. These are usually very large funds which are for the joint benefit of their members. They are managed by managerial companies, which, for a small percentage of the entire fund, carry on detailed research in particular industries and companies and in the general economy. Wholesale investment saves commission costs and research expenses. Some have done dramatically well and some disastrously. A consultation with a well-informed broker can be helpful here in obtaining information about the most advantageous mutual funds. You should know that some mutual funds are more "loaded" than others; that is, you must pay them certain sales charges.

The selection of a particular mutual fund is by no means easy; probably the best approach is an experimental one which includes participation in a number of different funds. Many mutual funds and brokerage concerns distribute analyses of the records of mutual funds, although many of these analyses reflect some degree of bias.

In theory, mutual funds should be an ideal investment vehicle in permitting diversification and affording a high level of investment skill to investors too small to obtain this skill elsewhere. In practice, however, this has not always been the case. One problem is that mutual funds are so large that when such funds start buying the stock of a particular company, it automatically goes up, but when they start selling, its decline is accelerated by the very volume of sales. However, with very astute management and a distribution of sales in time and space, this can be overcome.

A more serious problem is that many of the funds simply do not pay their research people well enough. Some years ago, we had to handle a claim of an executive against one of the largest mutual funds. This executive was taken out of a good job and given a fat contract to do strategic planning for the fund in question. It became apparent that the fund spent much more on its sales department than it did on its research department. A first recommendation was to reverse the ratio and spend much more money on research.

Unfortunately, sales personnel controlled the company, and our executive was promptly fired; but the fund voluntarily paid a very large amount in settlement rather than risk the publicity of a lawsuit.

Of course, this is not true of all mutual funds, particularly the "no load" funds, which pay no sales commission. Nevertheless, a great many mutual funds have done more poorly than the market as a whole. Only a relatively few have, over a period of five or ten years, done better than the market. These few are gems to be highly treasured.

The sources of data on mutual funds are: *Standard & Poor's Stock Guide, Institutional Investor Magazine,* and *Mutual Fund Digest.* A conscientious and vigorous investor should check the records of these funds and obtain if possible a chart going back five or more years, comparing the performance of the given fund to the Dow Jones averages, Standard & Poor's 500, and other comparatives mentioned above.

For obvious reasons, we cannot mention the "gem" funds, particularly because the record may not be the same by the time the reader gets her eyes on these words. You have to find them yourself or pay someone to do it. Stockbrokers are loath to do it, since on "no load" funds they receive no commission; but if you have an account with a stockbroker, you can often obtain such help.

After you have made the comparison, start with small investments and go on from there.

If you have substantial funds to invest, it might be well to employ an investment consultant. These range all the way from large national organizations which give advice to the holders of millions of dollars of securities down to individual consultants with only a few clients, with whom a highly personalized relationship is maintained. Usually, although not always, their charges are based on the amount invested plus some minimum charge and a declining percentage charge if investments are larger. Some consultants will not handle funds of less than $250,000; others will handle from $100,000 up; and still others will accept a figure as low as $10,000.

Another possible method is to try the services of a trust company. Trust companies make their own investment decisions for their trust or operate in coordination with investment consultants or even individual cotrustees. The skills of the investment departments of different trust companies vary highly. Here, too, it is important to know not only the organization but particular individuals. Trust companies are necessarily more conservative than other investment consultants. This can be a virtue, but not always. A number of trust companies now run what are called "common trust funds," which handle, as a unit, small funds which separately would be too small to warrant the attention that a large fund receives.

You cannot put any security away in your vault and forget it. We have seen some (all too rarely) securities go from $1 a share to $500 a share in ten years, but this does not mean that all securities should be held for ten years. A stock which went from $1 to $500 a share should have been watched all the way along the line. Someone said that eternal vigilance is the price of financial freedom, particularly in the stock market.

"Do I *have* to watch the market as well as hire an expert?" has been asked of us frequently. The answer to this is, "Yes."

You should get at least a monthly report from your stockbroker or investment adviser. You should request that the adviser compare his or her performance with the balance of the market, such as the Dow Jones averages, or other criteria such as A. G. Becker & Co., and the Weisenberger indices, and Standard & Poor's 500, which can be obtained from any stockbroker.

Now we come to the final question, the timing of your buying and selling. Assuming that the stock of a given company represents a good acquisition, or assuming that you have decided to dispose of shares you already hold, just when should this be done? The upswing or downswing in the price of a particular stock depends to a degree on the company itself and the changing opinion as to its earnings prospects, and on the market in general. Some shares will always resist the general action of the stock market, but the general trend should always be considered. The ideal, of course, is to follow Rothschild's famous goal of "buying cheap and selling dear."

There is a moderating factor that helps to avoid doing just the opposite, which is called "dollar averaging." This is how dollar averaging works. You decide not to try to catch the market or particular stock at its top or at its bottom, but to spread the risk. If you decide to invest $10,000 in all and to invest it all in the stock of a particular company (a not necessarily wise concentration), instead of calling up your broker and buying $10,000 worth of the stock, you buy instead, $500 worth of its stock every month for twenty months. When you start, if the stock is selling at $50 a share, you will buy ten shares in the first month. (10 X $50 = $500). Suppose it stays at $50 for the next twelve months, you will continue buying ten shares a month. If, after a year, the stock has gone up to $100 a share you will buy in that month five shares only (5 X $100 = $500). If in the fifteenth month it has dropped to $10 a share, you will buy fifty shares.

The same process can follow in reverse order if you are selling the stock, by selling a fixed dollar amount of shares over a given number of months. If the stock is selling at $100 a share and you are disposing of it at the rate of $500 a month, you will sell five shares, and if it is down to $10, you will sell fifty. Of course this is not necessarily an ironbound decision, and if the president of the company absconds with all its cash, it doesn't mean that you should continue to buy or sell in installments. But as a basic approach, dollar averaging has the virtue of a conservative spread of action in the stock, and it also tends to limit unduly impetuous or hunch buying or selling. It is apt to cut down the number of shares acquired at any given time and thus increase your aggregate commission cost (this is one of the virtues of investing through an investment company or group, which tends to offset the disadvantage of grouping together a number of individuals). But in any case it is a moderating factor.

Sometimes it is possible to get a stock at its very inception. We need hardly say that money must not be frittered away in a large number of miscellaneous "venture capital" situations. But, occasionally, there is an opportunity to get into something at the beginning. Apart from real estate, this has probably been the most fruitful source of the very large American fortunes.

If you do start on something that is brand new, such as a new type of camera, talk to an officer of the Small Business Administration, which maintains offices in most large cities. Talk to your attorney and to your investment consultant. But if you do make such an investment, look to our chapter on "Lending It," so that if things do go bad, as is the case with most new ventures, you can, at least, deduct your lost investment from your taxable income. It is particularly worthwhile, however, for executives to keep their eyes open for research and development opportunities and to marketing enterprises in areas where they have expertise, but which are not so close to their main business as to create a "conflict of interest." Never, never go into a small new venture without having your own lawyer check over the documents.

A term with which you should be familiar is "buying on margin." This means borrowing (usually from the stockbroker) part of the purchase price of the stock. During the wild stock-market inflation of the twenties, people plunged into stock market investments putting in only 10-percent capital or some other absurdly low proportion of their own money. Naturally, this amplified profits *IF THE STOCK WENT UP,* as most were doing. If you had $100 to invest and stock was selling $100 a share and you bought outright one share, and the price of the stock went up to $200, you could sell at a gain of $100. But if you bought on margin, you might be able to invest $100, borrow $900, and buy ten shares of stock. Then if the stock went up to $200, your profit would be $1,000 rather than $100. This was fine as long as the stock market kept going up. But if the stock went down eight or nine or ten points, your own investment would be exhausted and the people who loaned you the $900 would get worried and call for more "margin," that is, more of your own money. You might be able to scrounge around and get another $100, but then if the market went down another ten points, you'd get a call for more "margin." If you didn't have it, you would be sold out, and your investment would be totally wiped out. This would accelerate with the decline in the market. Had you bought only one share of stock for $100 in cash, you could have survived a twenty-point decline. You would not be happy, but at least you could wait for the stock to come back.

The panic of 1929 and the early thirties was mostly precipitated by margin buying. Congress stepped in and gave the Federal Reserve Bank the power to limit the percentage you could borrow against the purchase of stock. This percentage varies from time to time. If you want to be conservative, and we advise you so to be, limit your gains and limit your losses by avoiding margin buying or, except in the case of extreme and unexpected emergencies, don't borrow on the security of stock which you have held. If you don't have it, sell your stock and either take your loss or give up your chance for profit, and take care of the emergency. Don't "play" the stock market unless you can afford to.

Stocks are marketed at three different levels: closely held corporation; over the counter; and listed on the American Stock Exchange or the New York Stock Exchange, or others.

1. *Closely Held*—If the stock of a company is held by one person, one family, or a small group of individuals, it is a "closely held corporation." This has the advantage of having a concentration of management in what we will hope are skilled hands. Generally it is unwise to invest in a closely held corporation without a buy-out agreement, which can be activated should you retire, die, or have to liquidate. The tax law has special provisions providing for the accumulation of funds for such "buy-out" purposes. You should call on the services of an attorney, accountant, insurance agent, and trust officer to set up

a "buy-sell" program to provide in advance for such contingencies. Otherwise, your estate may be taxed on stock which the government claims is very valuable but which your heirs can't sell. In the chapter on insurance we quote the opinion in the *Emeloid* case, which explains how important insurance is when held for such purposes.

The chapter on retirement talks about ESOP, which is a tax-favored plan for buying up stock for the benefit of employees. All corporations should consider these programs, but closely held ones particularly so.

2. *Over-the-Counter Stock*—Frequently, when corporations reach an appropriate size or where the need for a liquid market is observed, a closely held corporation will issue new shares, which are sold to the public. This is usually done through an investment banking house or the investment banking department of a stockbrokerage firm. Sometimes a financial institution, such as a bank or insurance company, will buy the stock en bloc. Until such shares reach a status which entitles them to be listed on a stock exchange they are called "over-the-counter" stock. This is a physical statement of how they are traded as contrasted to the trading arenas in stock exchanges. Some investment consultants or stockbrokers concentrate on locating over-the-counter securities that have substantial growth potential. Frequently these represent excellent growth investments, but because of the relatively small number of shares available and the relatively small market, they partake of a greater risk in many (but not all) situations, as contrasted with listed securities.

3. *Listed Stock*—Finally, when securities reach a certain maturity, management demonstrates experience and reliability, and the number of traded shares are large, stock can graduate from over the counter to the point where it is traded on a national exchange, such as the New York Stock Exchange or the American Stock Exchange. These are called "listed shares."

If you need to borrow money on stock (see prior comments on this risky procedure), it is easier to do so with listed shares. Listed shares are the aristocrats of the corporate stock field, but that by no means suggests that they are immune to loss or more prone to gain. It mostly means that large aggregations of capital, such as mutual funds, will be more willing to purchase them. This means that the stock market may go up rapidly due to interests from large mutual funds, but it also means that it can go down just as rapidly if the mutual funds or other institutional buyers, such as pension funds, become disenchanted with them.

Two other terms require explanation. These are procedures that have existed for many years but only recently have become popular. They are "puts" and "calls."

A "put" is a contract whereby A (issuer) agrees, within a stipulated period of time, say 120 days, to buy a stipulated security for a stipulated price. A (issuer) might agree to buy from B (owner) the stock of the XYZ Corporation on the demand of B (owner) within 120 days at $100 a share. A (issuer) receives a very moderate payment from B (owner) for taking this risk. If the stock goes down to $90 within the stipulated period of time, B (owner) will call on A (issuer) to pick up the stock at $100 a share and A (issuer) is bound so to do. This can be advantageous to A (issuer) because if the stock remains level, or goes up, owner can retain the premium without spending any money. It then becomes a good source of income. On the other hand, there is a chance of being walloped with a big loss. On a basis somewhat comparable to margin buying, it is a means of getting into the stock market and profiting by an increase in the price level of the selected security.

A "call" is almost the reverse of a put. Suppose X (owner) owns some stock of the ABC Company which is selling at $100 a share. X (owner) takes the position that the stock will go up but is willing to improve the current income by agreeing to give Y (issuer) an option to purchase this stock, again within a stipulated period of time, for $110. If the stock does not go up to $110 within this stipulated period of time, let us say 120 days, Y (issuer) obviously will not exercise the option. If the stock has gone up but only to $105 it is cheaper for Y (issuer) to buy the stock on the market at $105 than to turn around and give X $110. But if the stock goes up to $120, within the time frame, then Y (issuer) will call for the stock and pay X (owner) $110 for it, having an immediate profit of $10, less the premium the owner paid when purchasing the call. While X (owner) may be disappointed in having to give up this stock, there will be the advantage of the use of the premium that the issuer paid. X (owner), of course, will sell the call only if in the judgment of X (owner) the price of the stock will not increase that rapidly. By selling calls, X (owner) can add to the dividend the premium paid by the ABC stock, and thus significantly improve the cash position.

Both puts and calls are really conservative steps which protect the stockholder while buying a put or selling a call. They are speculative on the part of the person who issues the put or buys the call. The first is betting that the stock market will not go up and the second is betting that it will go up.

It is a cheaper and easier way to profit (or lose) by fluctuations in the stock market.

We do not recommend venturing into this novel field without a good deal of study and consideration and without the guidance of an investment adviser whose success has been proven with other people, but they are procedures which, if you have substantial stock positions, you should know about.

General rules to consider before entering the stock market

1. Do not make substantial purchases of stock unless you are prepared to hold the stock for at least five years or to take a loss if you need to liquidate during a decline.

2. Do not buy stock until you have an adequate fund that is really liquid, such as deposits in savings institutions, the cash value of an insurance policy, or to a lesser degree, government or corporate bonds.

3. Do not invest in the stock market individually until you have weighed the possibility of participating through a tax-favored route, such as a profit-sharing trust or a variable annuity pension plan.

4. Do not invest income dollars in the stock market without having thoroughly explored the availability and comparable risk and growth factors of more tax-deductible investments, such as Subchapter S corporations or SBIC shares. (See chapter 5, "Lending It.")

5. Be extremely cautious if your primary goal is current income. Investment in the stock market should be made almost always in terms of increased income or gain in the future. If current income is what you need, you will probably do better with fixed-income investments. In this connection, such tax shelters allowed against income as depreciation on real estate investments in rental properties should be limited to a portion of your capital as an inflation hedge.

6. Do not invest even capital dollars in the stock market without the prior training and experience which we shall discuss at the end of this chapter.

The foregoing rules are all negative. They are all

related in their application to your own particular situation. They do not mean that you should not buy stock at all, but they do mean that the amount of investment and the form of investment should be very carefully considered by you in the light of their application to your particular situation.

In the long run, however, the really key question is a proper, effective analysis of the position of a particular company. This gives you an idea as to the virtues of buying or selling such common stock but also will help evaluate convertibles, preferred stock, and even the debt securities of that company. Here are ten key points in the valuation of the stock of a particular company. We advise that you learn them well and start applying them yourself.

1. *Earnings,* preferably should be moving steadily ahead with no interruption or only occasional slowing down. Cyclical peaks and troughs for earnings make the securities of these companies suitable only for professional trading.

2. *Revenues,* when moving ahead at a good clip over a considerable number of years demonstrate that the company's products and/or services are in growing demand and that the company's management is doing its homework.

3. *Net Equity Per Common Share (also called "Book Value")* should be growing consistently, reflecting a growth in earnings achieved without leveraging debt, which can always be a two-edged sword.

4. *Steady and Substantial Addition to Plant and Equipment* sets the stage for *continued* growth in earnings for the years ahead. This assures us that management is upgrading and modernizing facilities for efficient operation, improving the competitive position of the

company, and facilitating penetration of new markets. A concomitant benefit is the increase in the *replacement value* of new plant and equipment due to the steady inflation. Sooner or later this will be reflected in the common stock price. Another benefit is the growth in depreciation charges which shelter future income from federal and state taxation. When analyzing additions to plant and equipment, it is important to check the figure against any possible *growth in long-term debt* during the same period. If the additions to plant and equipment are matched by a growth in such debt, we are much less impressed because that dangerous leverage factor comes in again. When figuring any increase in debt we always look at net working capital as well, because any increase in that figure for the years covered is entitled to be deducted from the increase in debt to get the true picture. Where additions to plant and equipment have been made from cash flow *without* any increase in long-term debt, this is the most favorable sign.

5. *Price/Earnings Ratio,* derived by dividing the current price of the stock by the earnings per share should be modest, preferably low. Thus a stock selling at forty times earnings has often been punished severely as styles change and economic swings take place, while stocks available at five to ten times earnings, and particularly when the other factors listed above are favorable, have often been the springboard for stock market success.

6. *Current Assets* should be well in excess of current liabilities, with a strong cash segment of current assets very attractive. When cash or equivalents equal or surpass all current liabilities we have a very promising picture. Receivables can be considered next in im-

portance, but we never like to try to balance
out large current liabilities with the major
help coming from the "inventory" item in
current liabilities. When cash plus receivables
exceed all current liabilities we feel comfortable. Otherwise, we feel troubled.

7. *Cash Flow* per share should be generous when
    measured against the price of the stock. These
    are the stated earnings plus depreciation and
    other charges added back to reflect actual
    cash available for company purposes. A large
    cash flow means the company will not neces-
    sarily have to enter the market for additional
    capital when conditions are poor, unduly in-
    creasing the costs of securing that capital. A
    large cash flow also facilitates dividend in-
    creases and generally allows management to
    function well in all areas of product develop-
    ment, efficiency betterment, etc., instead of
    putting a great deal of effort into simply get-
    ting the cash to run the business.

8. *Dividends* should show a steady, even if un-
    spectacular, increase because, sooner or later,
    a rising dividend pay-out will increase the
    chances of the common stock rising in the
    marketplace.

9. *Long-Term Debt* should not show substantial
    increases over a period of years, and one
    should compare the yearly interest charge to
    service that debt with net income (not cash
    flow). If debt service charges are anything
    near as large as net income we would begin
    to be alarmed for obvious reasons. Any dip
    in earnings would get the company into
    trouble.

10. *The Price of the Stock* should not have soared
    recently. Even when all other factors out-
    lined above are favorable, a heady rise may
    have weakened the internal technical position

of the stock, making it vulnerable to a general market retreat, even when earnings, etc., continue to move ahead.

All the factors we have just enumerated are stated *directly* in the *Standard & Poor's Stock Reports,* which cover the New York Stock Exchange, American Stock Exchange and Regional Stock Exchanges, and Over-the-Counter, or just about every stock with a public market. Securing one of these reports on any individual company from one's broker will enable the investor to check off *every one* of the items we have discussed.

As another step, the investor should write to the company (address on the Standard & Poor's report) for a copy of their last annual report and proxy statement and read it carefully. There often is a wealth of information in such a report, including more detailed statistical studies covering the last decade, further detailing all the items we have outlined.

REAL ESTATE

As we said at the start of this chapter, do not put all your eggs in one basket. In addition to investing in the stock market, an investor can also go into real estate. This can be raw acreage or improved land. Rental real estate is often an ideal investment solution. It means rental from land that has been improved by income-producing assets placed upon it, such as apartment houses, shopping centers, office buildings, residences, and industrial plants. There are several reasons why these investments are excellent.

Rentals are more secure than dividends, and real estate more secure than stock. Dividends do not have to be paid, as we have already described. They become payable only when a board of directors elects to pay them. On the other hand, rental required to be paid by a lease is a debt obligation and must be paid or the tenant will face eviction or bankruptcy. Moreover, the liquidation of a lease comes before payments to stockholders if business is bad. It is for just this reason that stockholders are entitled to share in the growth of the company to an extent beyond the average landlord and why stocks may make a person rich, while rentals from real estate may leave her secure and maybe rich, as well.

Rental real estate has one great advantage and that is the depreciation which the tax law allows the owner of the building. As a building (or piece of equipment) grows older it depreciates, that is, it loses in value. A building is said to have a certain life expectancy. Let us assume that a building has a life expectancy of 33 1/3 years and cost $100,000. Theoretically, at the end of 33 1/3 years the building will have no value at all. It will be wholly depreciated. The investor is allowed to deduct from the rent a sum which offsets the loss of capital value. In this case the allowance would be $3,000, which means that if you as the landlord are receiving an annual rental of $10,000 you will have to pay tax on only $7000. Theoretically, you would be allowed to set aside $3000 in each of the 33 1/3 years of expected life, so that at the end of the time you would have been able to recover your $100,000 investment without tax. In actual fact, however, it is entirely possible that at the end of the 33 1/3 years the building instead of being valueless may be worth as much as $60,000. The building may have been kept in good repair, and the value of the real estate may have increased more rapidly than the years have cut down its business value. In such a case, the depreciation that has been taken by the owner has reduced her basis (her original investment) of $100,000 to zero. Under present law, if the building is sold for $60,000 this would represent a capital gain. This would mean that ordinary tax deductions at a high rate become capital gains, taxed at a low rate. Moreover, the tax law permits taking depreciation on a higher rate in the start, for example, $4,500 in the first year, and lesser amounts thereafter. If, as usually occurs, you buy a building with a high mortgage (sometimes 80 percent or even more), the tax savings may be greater than cash outlay.

Rental opportunities are extremely difficult to find, and the investor may have to exercise considerable patience and willingness to move rapidly when an opportunity does come along. Decisions should only be made, however, after adequate investigation by a lawyer of the terms of the lease and the credit of the tenant and the inherent real estate value. The long-range trend of real estate values must be checked out very carefully, and the credit rating of the tenant and subtenants must also be checked. The investor may have to establish relations with an astute builder who can find good locations and good tenants and who, as a reward for the investor's financial backing, will provide an opportunity for this type of excellent yield.

Remember that if more rapid depreciation is taken in earlier years, the rate of depreciation will decrease in later years. In that case the owner should make sure that she can sell out or refinance on satisfactory terms after a period of ten years, when the depreciation becomes less favorable. For the average widow or single woman, well-selected rental property is one of the best investment possibilities available. From an economic point of view an astute real estate consultant and a successful builder can be among the best business friends a woman can have.

An excellent investment for a young couple to look for is a two-family home. If one can be found on advantageous terms, the owners can live in half and rent the other half. The rent on half the house would be taxable income. But they would receive a deduction for depreciation on half of the cost of the house, even though they had not put up much cash. Of course the land itself could not be depreciated, but only a small portion of the purchase price in many cases is allocated to this factor. If, in addition, the purchaser has a mortgage, the interest on the mortgage is also deduc-

tible. Such an investment, in addition to the tax benefits, has the advantage of a reasonably assured income
and the likelihood of a capital gain after a brief period
of time or after ten years, depending on developments
in the area. No other investment available to a couple
with restricted means could possibly offer so good an
opportunity for a capital appreciation, except an investment in some very small company with a remarkable
future growth. The opportunities in trading up on income-producing real estate of modest proportions
purchased at bargain prices represents a major opportunity for capital growth on the part of an individual or
a couple in the lower-middle or lower income brackets.

Be sure to check out the neighborhood, the schools,
available public transportation, and the real estate tax
situation. Also, whether or not corporations are moving
their plants and headquarters into or out of the area.

Unimproved real estate, or raw acreage is also something to be considered for investment purposes. This
can be on the outskirts of a great city or in the middle
of a desert. Innumerable fortunes have been won and
lost in the purchase and sale of such land. Next to
the oil industry, probably nothing lends itself so easily
to misrepresentation as this area of business activity.
But this does not mean that we should close our eyes
to its opportunities. The first question to ask is, How
much is the demand for the land going to increase?
Some years ago, you could hardly give land away in
Danbury, Connecticut because its main industry—hat
manufacturing—moved away. But in Danbury there
was a large pool of available skilled labor. Gradually,
electronics companies moved in to take up this pool,
and new plants, like Union Carbide, began to spring
up. Today, Danbury is enjoying one of the greatest
real estate booms in the country.

Raw acreage is something you can go out and see
for yourself. Either buy your land yourself or combine
with a group of friends and set up a small syndicate
with enough money between you so that you can

acquire diversified parcels in a promising area. The diversification is necessary because there is always the possibility that new growth will be concentrated in one neighborhood and bypass another. Nobody can tell with complete assurance which neighborhood it will be.

Let us suppose you have found a piece of unimproved real estate or raw acreage in an area attractive to you, and that the land is expected to double in value in the next five years, and meanwhile carries nominal local real estate taxes. Here is where a significant tax decision must be made, involving the principle of leverage. In simple language, this means that you have to decide whether you want to buy the land outright or buy it subject to a mortgage on which you pay interest. This kind of acreage can be bought in some parts of the country subject to a mortgage with a long period of time in which to pay it off. Sometimes no payment has to be made on the principal of the mortgage for five years, sometimes not for several, sometimes not for ten. The leverage comes from the fact that interest is tax deductible and a little cash goes a long way. But real estate should be part of every well rounded portfolio.

Leverage applies to almost every form of investment. It merely means that you use borrowed money in making an investment with a relatively small commitment of your own funds. Margin buying on the stock market is another example, and you can borrow a portion of the purchase price of the stock, using the stock itself as security or collateral. The impact of leverage is that if the property goes up in value you make more money because the borrowed funds have permitted you to buy a larger amount of the particular investment than you would be able to purchase if you were to use only your own cash. However, if the property goes down in value and you are not able to put up more collateral or meet the installment payments which are usually required in a transaction involving a loan, the loan may be foreclosed; or if your margin ("collateral": your "security") is inadequate and you receive a margin call for more collateral, you might be sold out by the lender and lose your own cash. Thus, leverage increases your gains if the value of the property goes up and also enlarges your risk if the value goes down.

That is why a woman with children in high school should consider real estate sales as not only a source of high commission income, but as the equivalent of a college course on real estate as an investment.

5
Lending It

When you think of lending money, you usually think of lending money to your son or daughter or to a friend to tide them over some emergency. This is the kind of lending that you do as a favor for someone in a tight spot. But you can also lend for profit. In both cases, however, there is a good way to lend and many bad ways. When you lend as a favor, you should at least do it in a way that costs you the least, both financially and personally. Lending can make as many enemies as it can friends.

When you lend money, particularly to a friend or family member, it is important that you get a promissory note. There are several reasons for this:

First, it will prevent future disputes, particularly if the borrower dies or becomes unfriendly (as borrowers usually do). Also, it indicates that the advance was a real loan and not a gift.

The note should be negotiable. Below is a typical example.

May 10, 1979
The undersigned hereby promises to pay to the order of Jane Doe, $1,000.00 on the first day of September, 1980, with interest at 6%.

_____

Robert Roe

The words "to the order" are very important because you may want to take this note to your bank and discount it, that is, for a fee have them pay you in advance and be substituted for you as payee. These words make the note "negotiable." The bank will not accept the note if it doesn't have these words or, alternatively, "pay to the order of bearer."

If it is decided that the obligation will be paid in ten installments, you should then get ten notes with consecutive monthly dates on them, but then you should have on either the face of the note, or on the reverse side of the note, the following language:

This note is one of a series of ten notes. If there be default continuing for ten days in the payment of any note in this series, the entire balance unpaid shall come due immediately.

Also, the notes should provide the following:

In the case of default of payment of the within note or interest, the maker of the note shall be obligated to pay all legal fees or cost of collection.

This should be on all notes, whether installment notes or a single note.

Remember that if you get a note from a corporation, you cannot sue the individual who controls the corporation if the corporation defaults. If possible, on any corporate note, get the endorsement of the individual who may have more resources than the corporation. This endorsement is worded thus:

Payment endorsed and guaranteed by John Jeffreys.

When you lend to friends or family, you do not necessarily want to make a profit, but in all likelihood you would like to make it in the most tax-favored form. Suppose you want to lend your son $10,000 to get started in a business or to expand an enterprise. What happens if he cannot repay you, either because his business venture fails, or he becomes disabled? You have heard of "business bad debts" and wonder if you can get a tax deduction. It is true that business bad debts are fully deductible from taxable income, but the catch is that you, the issuer of credit, have to be either in the business of lending money or be in a commercial enterprise where sales on credit are a part of a business procedure. Only if you are in this position and make a loan which becomes totally uncollectible, and you can show that the borrower is totally without credit and never will be able to repay you, only in this case will the Treasury Department allow you to treat it as a "bad debt."

There is also something called a "nonbusiness bad debt." Suppose you lend your daughter $10,000 to maintain her while she writes a novel and after a while you come to the conclusion that she will never be able to repay you, can you treat it as a "nonbusiness bad debt?" Since 1978, the Treasury says that in this case you can take a $3,000 deduction each year until the debt is repaid. In other words, you can take a $3,000 deduction for each of three years, and a $1,000 deduction for one year, making up the total loan of $10,000. But these deductions do not really compensate you for the loss of cash. You may not even need the deduction in your tax bracket. You may come up with the great idea that you can use the deduction to offset a capital gain. For example, you may decide to sell some stock at a profit, which will give you a capital gain. You know that capital gains are taxable, so you think you can use the deduction to make up for the tax on the capital gain. Without going into the complicated computations, this procedure does not generally work out too well. In fact, the balancing of a "nonbusiness bad debt" with a capital gain may involve a tax loss.

In addition, the government may claim the debt was not proved to be uncollectible. In any event, a loan is apt to be a difficult element in a tax program. But there are several methods for lending money to a relative or a friend which can be more effective.

Since the Revenue Act of 1978, there is an added reason why you should not lend money for business investment to a member of your immediate family (direct ancestor, direct descendant, husband, wife, sister, or brother). Under the provisions of Section 465, as amended in 1978, a business deduction may not be taken by the borrower even if the money is lost in the business (except in the real estate business). This leaves the borrower still legally owing the money but unable to take a tax loss. Of course, this results in the reverse if *you* are the borrower and a member of your immediate family is the lender.

The way to avoid this is to use one of the three procedures now to be mentioned, e.g., investing the money in a Section 1244 corporation, a Subchapter S corporation or a limited partnership in which your relative has a share.

Getting back to your son to whom you have lent $10,000 for a business use, there are three ways in which you can deduct the loan. You ask him to set up his business as a "1244 corporation" (Section 1244 of the Internal Revenue Code). It would be wise to ask a lawyer to do this for you. As a matter of fact, either the borrower or the lender can set up the corporation. Either way it will meet the technical requirements of the Internal Revenue Code. What you do is to provide in the organization papers of the corporation that you want the option to qualify under Section 1244 if it should be necessary. If the loan is made to a corporation with this option, then if the corporation becomes insolvent and has to liquidate, or if the stock has to be sold at a loss, the loss will be deductible from ordinary income. In this way, if things go bad, the loss at least can be tax deductible. (In legal language this is "the election to qualify under Section 1244.") The form your loan takes is to use the $10,000 to purchase stock in the corporation.

Another form of organization which gives deductibility is a "Subchapter S corporation." In this case, also, you use the $10,000 to purchase stock. If this also turns out to be a loss situation, then the entire amount that any stockholder has put into the purchase of stock becomes deductible. A private individual who is not in the business, but who is a stockholder, may take this deduction as a business expense. Even if you are not in any business at all, you can deduct the loss as a "business expense." If the deduction exceeds the amount of a stockholder's income, she, the investor, has the benefit of what is called a "carry back" or a "carry forward." This means that she can go back and collect taxes paid in previous years (i.e. obtain a tax refund). If the back taxes are exhausted, she can carry the loss forward and apply it against future taxes.

There are several disadvantages with those corporations, however. Suppose they make money instead of losing it, then the money that is made is taxed personally to the stockholders, whether or not dividends are declared. So you find yourself in a position where start-up expenses are deductible, but the profits are taxed as ordinary income. The way out of this dilemma is to change from a Subchapter S to a regular corporation when success knocks at the door. If you do this you cannot requalify for five years. In a later step, you can exchange it for stock of a large and successful corporation. In this way your corporation is acquired by the large corporation and your son can have an employment contract as part of the deal. And in addition you have gotten out of your corporation what you put in, plus a profit. This has been the road to riches for the lucky investor who invests *deductibly* and ends up with marketable capital stock. As a matter of fact, the Subchapter S procedure is equally good for someone who wants merely to set up their own business.

A further fine point of the Subchapter S is that you must distribute the income correctly. This means that it must be distributed during the taxable year, or within sixty-five days afterwards. Also the distribution must be in cash or in a good check backed up by sufficient bank deposits so that it will be honored. If this is not done, there is a risk that the income will be taxed twice; first to the shareholders for the year in which it was earned, and then when it is eventually distributed.

A basic tax principle of Subchapter S corporations is that both gains and losses bear a direct relationship to the amount of stock you own. Let us say that one hundred shares were issued and you took fifty for your $10,000 and your son took fifty for his skill and organizational ability. (Incidentally, this type of corporation may have only one class of stock.) You each now own one half of the stock. In the event that the corporation goes broke, you may take a deduction for only half of your $10,000 investment. This would be the same if you owned a third, a quarter, or a tenth of the stock. You would take a deduction equivalent to the proportion of stock you own. You do not get a deduction fully equivalent to your loss.

If the Subchapter S corporation receives passive income, that is, interest, royalties, dividends, or rents, you must be very careful that it does not exceed 20 percent of the corporate income. If it does, you could lose the qualification for the Subchapter S and with it, your personal deduction.

A Subchapter S may not have a full-blown employee

benefit plan, but is treated the same as an individual setting up her own pension plan. This and the other limitations of a Subchapter S are discussed further in the chapter about retirement.

You may wonder, Why choose a Subchapter S corporation at all with its negative features? But it has one positive feature that makes it very worthwhile and that is that corporate salaries to management do not get taxed above 50 percent. Considering that taxes can go as high as 70 percent, this is a definite advantage.

We have already mentioned two ways to lend money to a son in a mutually helpful way, the first being the 1244 corporation, and the second the Subchapter S corporation. The third method is to set up a partnership. This does not have the tax advantage that the Subchapter S has with regard to the 50 percent tax ceiling on management salaries, but it has other advantages.

The form of partnership to set up for this purpose is a limited partnership which is an organization of two or more people. One or more of them will be general partners and one or more will be limited partners. The general partner (or partners) manage the partnership and are personally liable for its debts. The limited partner (or partners) invest capital and are not responsible for the debts of the partnership beyond the amount of capital they have invested. If the partnership goes badly and the capital is lost, the loss comes off ordinary income. This is a main difference between Subchapter income. In partnerships loss may be allocated per contract but in Subchapters only per stock held.

If your son, other family member, or friend looks to you for financial backing and their venture is, for example, a Broadway show, motion picture, oil and gas project, or a real estate development, you will find that the limited partnership route is one frequently used. One of the advantages is that the losses and income do not have to be shared strictly in accordance with investment. It can be provided that the income of a partnership must first go to the limited partners, until their investments have been repaid; and that afterwards, future income can be shared equally between the managers and the investors.

A further point to note about limited partnerships is that local law usually requires that they file a notice, and in some states, advertise as well, to notify creditors that they cannot look to the personal credit of the limited partners to pay any of the debts of the partnership.

Another point to note is that sometimes the partnership is set up so that the general partner is a corporation. The Internal Revenue Service puts severe limitations on this procedure and requires that the partnership itself must have adequate capital or the entire organization will lose the advantages of being a partnership. The major advantage is that losses can be taken as ordinary business losses and that depreciation and other tax deductions are fed through from the partnership to the individual partners in accordance with the partnership agreement.

One further point to clarify is that your investment (the original $10,000 we talked about) buys you an "interest" in the partnership.

In addition, a limited partner may be a trust set up for the benefit of a family member or the dependents of the investor. This means that as the property grows in value, some of the growth can pass, without gift or estate tax, to the trust (or trusts) for the benefit of future generations.

If a limited partnership strikes it rich, the income is also taxed to the individual partners. Sometimes this income is offset by depreciation and other deductions. If it is not, it is often worthwhile to convert the partnership into a corporation; and to exchange the corporate stock for that of a publicly held corporation which desires to acquire the now successful business.

Let us now take a jump into the ranching business.

We know of a family in a western state that owns a large ranch. They set up a limited partnership with trusts in it for family members. They simultaneously set up a corporation to manage the enterprise. It is an excellent form of organization to have a regular corporation manage your partnership business. General partners may also be officers of the corporation. The management corporation pays salaries to the people who do the work. In this instance the father and his son and daughter were workers along with various farm laborers. The corporation was also able, within the strict provisions of the Internal Revenue Service, to provide a pension and profit-sharing plan for the family workers, and the ranch foreman whose compensation had also the advantage of being "earned income" with a limited tax base.

The partnership leased its equipment and structures to the corporation. It also could lease, if it had them, patents or trade names. It is particularly useful to have the tangible side of the business owned by such a family partnership, with family trusts being operated by a corporation. This is the best of both possible worlds because the partners get the benefit of the allowance for depreciation and avoid a double capital-gains tax if tangible assets go up in value and are sold by the partnership. Investment in such a partnership is far better than just making a loan to a corporation or individual. Not only are the losses deductible if that occurs, but also gains can be taxed only once. It is also quite easy to go from the partnership form to the corporate form but very difficult to go the other way.

The net of all this is that if you are going to lend or invest money in a small, personalized enterprise, you should then consult your attorney and accountant and make the investment along the lines indicated above. If the loan is to a large institution, either government or corporate, an investment adviser will be an additional safeguard.

We turn to more sophisticated lending operations.

Lending for profit has been the bastion of big business, and a percentage point here and there can make the difference between big gains and big losses. A study of the following pages can make these techniques available to individuals.

A lending operation, not generally recognized as such, is done between the issuers and the purchasers of bonds. Women frequently purchase bonds because they believe them to be supersafe, but they do not see it as a lending operation in which *they* "lend" funds to the issuer, whether it is the United States government, one of the states, an agency of the state (such as the Port Authority of New York), a municipality or other local agency, or a corporation.

There is a tax distinction between government and corporate bonds, on the one hand, and municipal bonds ("municipals"), on the other hand. The interest paid on municipals is tax exempt from both federal and state authorities, whereas the interest paid on corporate and government bonds is not tax exempt. However, one state may tax the interest on the yield from the bond of another state. Now, in the case of municipals, if you buy a municipal bond with the face amount of $1,000 and pay only $700 for it, and later redeem it for $1,000, your gain of $300 is considered interest and not taxed. Because of this tax exemption, the yield on these bonds is usually less than on corporate bonds. In other words, because the interest is tax exempt, the issuers give you a smaller yield.

By contrast, a corporate bond is the note of a corporation acknowledging indebtedness in a stipulated amount and provides for repayment of the bond at maturity and pays interest usually in quarterly installments. The interest is not tax exempt and is treated as ordinary income. Such corporate bonds are secured by a mortgage on a corporate property, such as a plant, office building or equipment. If the investor (lender) has a mere promise of repayment, which is not secured by collateral, the obligation is called a "corporate debenture," rather than a corporate bond. (See comments on convertible bonds or debentures in the previous chapter on investments.)

While it may be a patriotic duty to buy United States government bonds, it is not necessarily a good investment from a strictly business point of view. Despite the security accorded a government bond, the value of the dollars which will be repaid at the end of a given time has been shrinking from inflation and will probably continue to shrink. The investor may lose as much in purchasing power and taxes as he gains from interest.

If you buy $500 worth of government bonds and five years later get $600 for the bond, the $100 profit is worth less in purchasing power than it was five years earlier. Besides, the $100 profit is considered a capital gain and is taxed as such. Another consideration is that the interest rate is expected to keep on increasing. Suppose you bought a bond that stipulated that it would pay 4.5 percent interest, and a year later the government issued new bonds offering 6 percent interest. You can see that your 4.5 percent bond would be less desirable as an investment. Consequently, its price would drop, and you would not be able to sell it for the same price as you bought it for, unless its maturity date were in the immediate future. No investor wants to be caught for any great length of time with a bond that carries a lower rate of interest than bonds issued later by the government, or any other issuer. This is why, despite their obvious safety, United States government bonds frequently sell below their face value, or in other words, less than "par." "Par" means that amount due on the bond at maturity. Accordingly, the investor can lose money if she is forced to liquidate at a discount before maturity. The loss can be avoided if (under the guidance of a real pro) bonds are bought in a series; each one maturing one year later than the earlier one. As the maturity date gets later, the yield goes up. Each annual maturity (the bond will be redeemed at par) will give you the current cash you may need.

Municipal bonds have the great advantage of having their income exempt from federal income taxes and frequently from state taxes as well. However, there are two disadvantages to keep in mind. Some municipalities, such as New York City, have lost their economic reliability in the public mind, at least to a considerable extent. This causes the bonds to be rated down (go below par) and thus anyone having to liquidate them may have to take a loss.

In fact, there is always the danger that someday a municipality will go into bankruptcy; and there could then be a long delay in collecting the amount due on the bond. There is no actual guarantee that you would ever collect, though there are some mutual funds that deal in municipal bonds that guarantee the payment of principal and interest, but even they do not guarantee that the interest rates won't go up, or the principal won't shrink from inflation, so that you may have to take a loss if you sell before maturity.

As we mentioned in connection with government bonds, when the interest rate goes up and a later issue of bonds pays a higher interest, it makes the earlier issued bonds less desirable, and their value goes down. Municipal bonds can go below par just as U.S. government bonds can. The unfortunate owner, if forced to sell early, then takes a loss.

Accordingly, the cautious investor in municipals looks for bonds which have a maturity date of five years or less. She can then just put the bonds away in her vault and wait for them to mature. This presupposes that no uninsured emergency will happen to her during those five years. The closer a bond gets to maturity, the less the discount, even if the interest rate is comparatively unfavorable. In fact, if the rate is unfavorable, it might be possible to pick up a bargain from a person forced to sell his municipal bonds at a discount. Then, if the bond is held to maturity, the new buyer not only gets tax-exempt interest, but also realizes a capital gain in the difference between the price paid for the bond and its full par value at maturity. Since capital gains are taxed at a lower rate this is a real advantage.

Also, the cautious investor looks to the source of credit of the municipal bonds. Bonds that are secured by the general credit of the state, municipality, or agency that issues them are called "general credit bonds" and may not be as safe as "revenue bonds," which are earmarked by the state, municipality, or agency for some special project like an income-producing factory. Your revenue comes directly from the income the project produces. The general credit bond can be infected with the ills of a sick state or municipality, but a revenue bond is an isolated venture and can remain immune.

The government has ruled out a marvelous scheme that investors dreamed up in which they borrowed money to buy municipals and claimed a deduction for the interest on the loan. This way they got deductible interest on the loan and tax-free income from the bonds. Now the tax law no longer permits the deduction of interest paid on a loan used to acquire or hold tax-exempt securities. This means it can be quite expensive to borrow using municipal bonds for collateral because the interest you will pay will not be tax deductible.

Nevertheless, municipals can be an excellent investment in an appropriate case. But you should buy through a stockbrokerage firm or dealer that specializes in municipal bonds.

There are now municipal bond mutual funds. They make it possible for the small investor to get a share in diversified issues. The investor also benefits from the investment counsel of the firm that manages the fund. Your investment consultant should be able to compare the aggregate safety and yield of a mutual bond fund with that of specifically selected bonds which you alone may own.

There are also companies which, for a very small

premium, insure the payment of interest and the principal amount of municipal bonds. While this insurance is reassuring, it does not protect you if the interest rate becomes lower than that of later bonds. In that situation, no matter how safe the bond may be, if you find that you have to liquidate, you will have to sell at a discount and take a loss. The insurance does not protect you on this score.

Throughout this book, we have talked about inflation. By the time you read the book, though, we may be in a recession, and that is a deflation. This is why we have tried to hedge our bets with regard to savings, loans, and investments and have advised against buying on too heavy a margin. But even if we are in a deflation, remember that the continuing trend over the decades has been clearly inflationary and that sooner or later inflation will come back to influence us.

6

Borrowing It

Borrowing money really is the other side of the coin of lending it.

Borrowing may be either from an institution or from an individual. The major institutional sources of loans are savings institutions, such as savings banks or savings and loan associations, commercial banks, insurance companies, credit associations (usually associated with an employer or union), fraternal organizations, and special agencies of the government, particularly the U. S. Government. The variety of loans available from Federal agency sources is so great that it is impossible to enumerate them all, but they include disaster, education and farm loans. Those which are most apt to apply to the average person are Veteran Administration loans for homes, FHA loans for multiple housing, and the like. Always check with the Government Information Service. Look it up in the phone book if you need money. The bank will also advise you on this score.

An invaluable source of loans for small businesses

is the Small Business Administration. At the present time, the Small Business Administration has millions earmarked to help women get started in or expand a business. Such loans are made by banks but on approval of the SBA are 90 percent guaranteed by that agency. Such loans are greatly favored by banks, since they permit the bank to make profitable loans with negligible risk. Moreover, you can get good business advice from the SBA.

Charge accounts and credit cards are a type of borrowing. Bank cards, like Master Charge and VISA, are in actuality a convenient way for you to get a loan. They give you a "credit line," which could be anywhere from $1,000 to $5,000, which means you can "borrow" up to the specified amount. Then every month you must repay a small percentage of the amount you owe, plus interest on the remaining balance. But this is a very expensive way to borrow or to purchase despite the convenience of spreading your payments over a long period of time. Compare this to a passbook loan. On the bank card, you could pay as high as 18 percent or more, but on a passbook loan, you could pay about 9 percent while at the same time your savings account was earning from 5 to 7 percent so your loan would only be costing you the difference: 9% (Interest cost of loan) − 6% (Interest earned account) = 3% (Actual cost of loan). Just figure out how much a new TV set would cost either way. There's a big difference between 18 percent and 3 percent.

$600 TV Set + $108 (18% Interest) = $708
$600 TV Set + $ 18 (3% Interest) = $618
Amount saved by using passbook loan $ 90

When you borrow, shop around for the lowest interest rate. Go to different banks. This is particularly important when you make a loan secured by tangible property, such as your home, your shop, or your automobile. The lending laws now require that the actual cost of interest be clearly stipulated. What looks like a 9-percent loan can end up being a 16-percent loan because the amount of interest for a year or some similar period can be taken off the amount of the loan which you are supposed to be receiving. Be very careful that your actual interest rate is explained to you in writing.

Before you borrow, check with an accountant or tax lawyer to make sure that your interest payments will be tax deductible. For example, interest on loans made to purchase tax-exempt bonds is not deductible. With certain limited exceptions, if you borrow more than three out of the first seven years' premiums on a life insurance policy, you lose the right to deduct the interest from your taxable income. After seven years you can borrow (depending on your age at the issuance of the policy) most, and sometimes all, of the premiums which could not be borrowed during the first seven years. Moreover, interest in excess of a given amount is nondeductible. The rules on this are extremely complicated and usually are changed with every new tax law. Therefore, before you borrow a substantial amount, check with your professional tax adviser.

It is important that you establish good credit before you really run into an emergency which requires a loan. It might even be a good practice to take a small loan for a short period from your savings institution or bank to make sure that your credit is good. But take it for a specific purpose because banks always want to know what you want the loan for. Lending institutions cooperate in keeping files on borrowers or potential borrowers. These list all adverse information about lawsuits, unpaid bills, and the like. If you apply for a loan and are turned down, you now have a right under federal law to get the credit report on yourself and, in fact, to see the entire file. If there is a mistake in the file or anything else which is unfair, you have a right to add to the file your own statement explaining this misinformation. Since this can be a lengthy process, it is wise to check out your credit status in advance of some urgent need for that credit.

A good, personal business practice is to make a personal financial statement for yourself once a year. This will give you a picture of where you stand financially. Then when the day comes that you need to have a loan, you will be ready with information that the lending organization requires. You will need to give less information when you open a charge account than when you apply for a loan from a bank, say, to put a new roof on your house, to buy a car, or to pay off an accumulation of personal debts.

Your personal financial statement consists of two parts: a balance sheet, and an income and expense statement. The balance sheet tells how much you are worth. By subtracting the total amount of what you owe (your liabilities) from the total of what you possess (your assets) you arrive at a figure called your "net worth." If you want to get a mortgage on a house you wish to purchase, the lending institution will be exceedingly interested in your net worth. They will also want to know about your income and expenses. Your income and expense statement will tell where you get your income from, and on what you spend it. In the left column you will list your income. In the right column you will list two kinds of expenses: fixed and variable. The fixed expenses are things like insurance payments, car payments, and, in fact, all payments in fixed amounts that are to be paid at stipulated times. The variables are items that must be paid for regularly, but which fluctuate in amount, like electric bills, phone bills, heating oil, and transportation.

When you subtract your total expenses (fixed and variable) from your total income, you will have left an amount available for savings, investments, or debt payment.

Often the greatest need for a loan is to pay for the cost of a higher education. Today, college costs are higher than ever before, but there are many financing opportunities available from federal and state governments, colleges and universities, and private organizations like unions, business, industry, foundations, churches, 4-H groups, and many more. Your first source of information is your child's high school guidance counselor. If you think you need aid, you should start inquiring at least one, and preferably two, full years before graduation. The most desirable loan has low interest and is long term. The National Direct Student Loan program offers needy students both low-interest and long-term loans. For information write to the financial aid office of the college you plan to attend. To find out about low-interest loans from private lenders that are guaranteed by the federal government, write to The Bureau of Higher Education, U.S. Office of Education, Washington, D. C. 20202. Commercial lending institutions offer loans at substantially higher interest rates than loans from noncommercial sources. Two non-commercial sources are United Student Aid Funds, Inc., 5259 North Tacoma Avenue, Indianapolis, Indiana 46220, and Tuition Plan, Inc., 575 Madison Avenue, New York, New York 10022. Also, some of the universities, like Yale and Duke, now have tuition-postponement loan plans that permit graduates to repay loans according to their post graduate earning power. The federal government offers a number of special loan programs in certain health fields like nursing, dentistry, optometry, pharmacy, and veterinary medicine. For information, write: Bureau of Health Professions, Manpower Education, Division of Physicians and Health Professional Education, National Institutes of Health, 9000 Rockville Pike, Bethesda, Maryland 20014.

Though low-interest and long-term loans are desirable when you borrow money, sometimes you have no choice but to pay a very high rate of interest in an emergency. Suppose there is a mortgage on your home that you have gradually reduced, and then some medical problem not adequately covered by insurance comes along and there is a desperate need for a large sum of cash. Perhaps you can increase your first mortgage if it has been faithfully decreased. To do so, however, might subject you to a higher interest rate than that stipulated in an earlier mortgage. Or, you might not be able to increase the mortgage or may not want to do so because of the increased interest rate. Sometimes it is necessary to take a second mortgage. Since the rights of the second mortgagee (the lender) are subordinate to those of the first mortgagee, and thus subject to greater risk, the interest rate on second mortgages can be very high. You want to make sure that you have the right to pay off the second mortgage ahead of schedule, without penalty, if your financial position improves. Second mortgages should be used only in the case of the most dire emergency and should be discharged as soon as possible. Otherwise, you probably will lose your home or shop.

A substitute for borrowing money to buy is now to arrange for the rental of what you need, such as an automobile, a computer, or the like. This setup can have tax advantages for both parties. Usually the lessor has borrowed the cost of the equipment from a bank, added on some more for himself and thus calculated the rental figure, so the rental is always predicated on an interest rate, even though the arrangement is not technically a loan. Before going into one of these transactions, be sure that you know what the interest factor, calculated in the rental, amounts to. Ask.

If you are going into business and want to use a loan for start-up capital and cannot obtain the loan from the usual business sources and must turn to friends or relatives, you will find them much more receptive if you set the loan up on a basis which, at least, will give them a tax deduction if you are unable to pay back the loan or if you have initial losses which are eventually followed by profits. The methods of doing this, with a great tax advantage to the lender, are discussed in the preceding chapter, "Lending It." These include Subchapter S corporations, Section 1244 corporations, and limited partnerships. By being helpful to your lender or investor in terms of taxes you will have a much more responsive audience when you ask for the loan.

Sometimes, if no other resources will work, you may be able to persuade a friend or relative to endorse, that is, guarantee your bank loan. This looks easy, but it is a trap to be avoided, since, if the endorser has to pay up on your loan, it will sour your relationship forever. It is much better to have someone use his own money or even borrow money and advance it to you in one of the tax-deductible fashions mentioned above. At least if the money is lost, he will save on taxes.

Remember that moderate loans, well calculated and well structured, are the very life blood of American business and justify a great deal of thought. Badly structured credit with extortionate interest rates can be one of the most destructive elements in your life.

INCOME AND EXPENSES

Income

GROSS SALARY/WAGES
(less payroll deductions) $_____

TIPS, BONUSES $_____

INTEREST OR DIVIDENDS $_____

INCOME FROM TRUSTS $_____

ROYALTIES OR RESIDUALS $_____

PROFIT FROM SALE OF ASSETS $_____

PROFIT FROM RENTAL REAL ESTATE $_____

GIFTS OF MONEY $_____

REFUNDS $_____

SOCIAL SECURITY BENEFITS $_____

PENSIONS $_____

ANNUITIES $_____

VETERAN BENEFITS $_____

UNEMPLOYMENT BENEFITS $_____

DISABILITY BENEFITS $_____

Total Income $_____

Fixed Expenses

RENT $_____

MORTGAGE AND LOAN PAYMENTS $_____

INCOME TAXES ($\pm$) $_____

INSTALLMENT PAYMENTS $_____

INSURANCE $_____

DUES (clubs, union, etc.) $_____

SPECIAL PAYMENTS:

   CHILD SUPPORT $_____

   ALIMONY $_____

   SUPPORT OF AGED RELATIVES $_____

Variable Expenses

FOOD $_____

UTILITIES $_____

TRANSPORTATION $_____

MEDICAL/DENTAL $_____

HOUSEHOLD MAINTENANCE $_____

CLOTHING & PERSONAL EXPENSES $_____

EDUCATION $_____

RECREATION $_____

Total Expenses $_____

Total Income $_____

Minus Total Expenses (fixed & variable) $_____

   **Amount Available for Savings, Investments
or Debt Payment** $_____

Assets

CASH $_____

STOCKS, BONDS $_____

KEOGH OR RETIREMENT ACCOUNT $_____

VESTED PENSION $_____

CASH SURRENDER VALUE OF LIFE INSURANCE $_____

OUTSTANDING PAYMENTS DUE YOU $_____

PATENTS, TRUST FUNDS, ETC. $_____

REAL ESTATE $_____

OTHER ASSETS:

   CAR $_____

   HOME FURNISHINGS $_____

   ART/ANTIQUES $_____

   TOOLS & EQUIPMENT $_____

Total Assets $_____

Liabilities

MONEY OWED:

    ON GOODS, SERVICES $_____

    INSTALLMENT CREDIT CONTRACTS
      (as for car purchase, etc.) $_____

    ON CASH LOANS $_____

TAXES:

    INCOME TAXES $_____

    PROPERTY TAXES (unless included in
      mortgage) $_____

REAL ESTATE:
    MORTGAGES $_____

    SPECIAL LOANS $_____

MISCELLANEOUS DEBTS $_____

Total Liabilities $_____

Net Worth—Assets Less Your Liabilities $_____

Assets $_____

Minus Liabilities $_____

Net Worth $_____

7

Insuring It: Life Insurance

Next to opening a savings account, the second most important financial step any woman or her husband can take is to purchase insurance. Savings and insurance programs are two of the most vital and significant elements of western capitalistic society, and *both* can be used to provide security in emergencies, *or* funds for a new car, a vacation, further education, or even to open a business.

A knowledge of how insurance works is an essential precondition for building a sound and economical insurance program. The selection of an insurance agent, an insurance company, and an insurance policy is one of the most important financial choices of a lifetime.

Most insurance purchased is on the life of a husband or a father because traditionally they have been the main source of support for themselves and their families. Now, with close to 50 percent of our work force female, it becomes important for women, also. Incidentally, it is not generally known that insurance on women is considerably cheaper than on men. Insurance is based only partially on your age. A woman pays about the same amount that a man three years her junior pays.

There is a great deal of confusion in the general public about the two main forms of life insurance, namely "term" and "permanent." Permanent is also called "whole life" or "ordinary." At first glance, most people prefer term because it appears to be cheaper. They make price the first consideration. They want to buy the greatest amount of protection for the least amount of money. But they overlook a few of the disadvantages of term insurance, one of them being that it is more costly *in the long run*.

The reason that it is more costly is that it is tied in with your age at the time you purchase it and is only issued for specified periods of time. Hence the use of the word "term." In its purest and earliest form it is only issued for one year at a time. This is "pure term." At the end of that year, if you want to continue the coverage, you must take a new medical examination and pay a higher premium because you are one year older. In other words, if you purchase term at age thirty, it is more expensive than if you take it at age twenty.

A slightly better form of term is "five-year renewable term." In this case the premium stays the same for five years, and you do not have to take a medical examination each of the five years. But even with renewable term, the policy terminates at the stipulated age. This age is at the end of the renewable period, such as five, ten or twenty years, or until age sixty-five or seventy. At some age when you might need it most, you find yourself without insurance. The premiums on renewable term are slightly higher than on pure term.

As stated, term insurance looks like a bargain, but the cost increases as age increases. Insurance companies developed "permanent insurance" as a way out of this trap. Most term insurance provides that you may convert the term policy into a permanent policy without taking a medical examination. In that event, the premium rate is based on your age at the time of conversion. For example, if you are thirty years of age and you buy a five-year renewable and convertible policy, at the end of five years if you then convert to permanent, the rate of premium will be based on age thirty-five, not age thirty. It is a fact that the net cost overall will be higher than if you had taken out permanent insurance at age thirty. Don't be misled by TV commercials offering sizable insurance for minuscule cost. They don't tell you their figures are based on age thirty or younger.

Permanent insurance has at least two advantages over term. First, it has no cutoff date. It lasts for life or as long as you continue paying the premiums. Second, it builds up a cash reserve for you. The way the insurance companies produce these advantages is to charge a level premium for the entire life of the policy. Part of each of these premiums is set aside in a reserve which the insurance company uses as an investment fund. In essence, term is a system of pay as you go, whereas permanent is a system where you pay in advance in the younger years of the policy. This so-called advance works for you in the insurance company investment fund. This fund really builds up. The rate of increase depends on the investment and administrative skills of the insurance company, at least in a "mutual" company. The existence of this investment fund means that the holder of a permanent policy has what is known as a "cash reserve" standing behind the policy. You might consider it as an enforced savings program. Insurance companies invest in a multitude of enterprises such as real estate, corporate loans, government bonds, and loans to their own policyholders. Term insurance enjoys no such reserve and thus has no such cash value.

The existence of this reserve does four things: First, you can use the cash reserve as security for a loan. The law requires the insurance company to lend to the policyholder of a permanent insurance policy at least 95 percent of the cash value. Banks are willing to lend up to 100 percent of the cash value. The availability of such cash value loans makes such policies an excellent source of emergency funds. The policyholder has here the closest to 100 percent security that our society provides. The interest chargeable by the insurance company on such loans is relatively low. Older policies were and still are limited to a 5 percent rate. Whatever your policy stipulates is permanently available to you. In many states, the rate has gone up to 8 percent (Connecticut is one example). But there are places where even on new insurance you pay only a 6 percent rate (Pennsylvania, for example). Some mutual companies pay lower "dividends" on low-interest policies. Others have a uniform scale. Check comparative rates. Subject to a very few highly technical exceptions, which you should check with a tax adviser, the interest is tax deductible. Moreover, you are not personally liable on these loans. They are only a charge against the policy, payable out of the insurance proceeds at death.

Secondly, if you want to discontinue a permanent policy, you merely surrender it and receive the cash reserve that has been building up for you. This sum is called the "cash surrender value," or merely the "cash value" of the policy. Naturally, if you surrender the policy, you forfeit the ultimate death benefit.

Thirdly, you have the option to use this cash value to convert the policy to a "paid-up" policy. This merely means that at some point along the way the cash value is enough to pay the full amount on the face of the policy.

And, fourthly, you can arrange to use the cash value to pay a premium that you may not be able to afford during some financial low in your life. This is called the "automatic premium payment" provision, and it is treated as a loan against your policy, and as in any other loan, interest is charged. You can reinstate yourself by paying off the loan, besides continuing to pay the premiums as they come up. The cash value will continue to build up. Of course, if you use up cash values to pay premiums and do not repay, at the time of death this will decrease the amount payable to your beneficiary.

Thus, permanent insurance, in addition to paying out when the insured dies, also provides emergency funds during life. This will be discussed in greater detail later on in the chapter. In the meantime, we will go further into the subject of term insurance by considering "renewable term."

As mentioned above, you may purchase five-year renewable term to avoid renewing your policy every year. This type of insurance is more expensive than pure term. The more term insurance resembles permanent insurance in its characteristics of permanency and a level premium rate, the closer the premium comes to the net cost of permanent insurance. (Net cost means the premium minus cash value increases and in some cases insurance dividends.)

There are also some policies which become "paid up" after a period of years, called "ten-pay life," where no premiums are payable after ten years, and "paid-up at (age) 65," and even "single premium" policies. Naturally, the premiums go up and up as fewer premiums must be paid.

Also, for a slightly increased premium you can buy a policy where the payment of premiums is waived if the insured becomes permanently disabled. Some policies even provide for the payment of income to the insured if he or she becomes disabled.

A form of insurance that is mostly term is called "group life." An employer, particularly of a large company, often provides "group life insurance." If the group is large enough, no physical examination is required, based on the theory that the mortality rate will be about the same as in the general population. The cost for the older participants is averaged with the cost for the younger ones. Sometimes, the employee is called on to contribute to the premium cost. This insurance seems very cheap indeed.

In actual fact, it can be very costly to rely entirely on such group term policies, instead of on individual permanent policies. For example, if you change your job and go to another company, you usually have to forfeit your policy, since no cash value has been building up for you as in permanent insurance. Even if you have been with a company for twenty or thirty years and are then fired, or retire, you will generally lose all those years of protection and have to start all over again with a new insurance program. On such retirement, etc., you can then convert the policy into permanent insurance. But the premium is at the attained age and is usually impossibly costly.

We suggest only two instances in which to buy term insurance. The first is when you need it only for a limited time, as, for example, when someone owes you a large amount of money and you fear that you will not get repaid if the person dies. In this instance, you can take insurance on the life of the person who owes you money in the amount of the debt. You have what is called an "insurable interest" in your debtor. In this way you get paid one way or the other. The second instance is if you are so limited in cash that you can buy insurance in no other way.

In both of these instances, however, you have the option of buying convertible term. You should do so in a first-class company and convert to permanent as soon as possible. In the first instance, this will be when the debt is paid off and you decide to continue the insurance, which you are permited to do. Convertible term may cost a little bit more than straight term in a less-favored company, but the difference is so negligible that it is worth incurring it so that when you can convert into a permanent policy you will be able to do so with a policy whose permanent net costs will be the lowest over a long period of time.

TWO TYPES OF INSURANCE COMPANIES

Life insurance companies are of two main types: mutual companies and stock companies. A mutual company is owned by its policyholders. A stock company is owned by its stockholders. A stock company is operated for the ultimate profit of its stockholders.

Life insurance is also in some cases issued by a government system, as with insurance issued to those in military service, or by savings institutions, or by a company owned by a large employer of tens of thousands of persons, and finally by fraternal associations or churches.

Traditionally, mutual companies charge higher premiums than stock companies, for the reason that stock companies have an extra reserve to fall back on, which comes from their stockholders. However, mutual companies return a portion of premiums to the policyholder as "dividends" at the end of each policy year. Since such dividends are really returns of excess premiums, they are tax free.

It is a matter of confusion to the public that mutual companies pay dividends whereas stock companies do not as such. As a stockholder in a stock company, you receive dividends as with any other stock company, but as a policyholder you have no contractual right to dividends, unless you may own what is known as a "participating policy." The fierce competition between mutual and stock companies motivates each mutual company to pay as high dividends as prudence allows, while stock companies either decrease premiums or offer participating contracts. The stock companies on their nonparticipating contracts pay no dividends but have lower premiums than a competitive mutual policy. The mutual companies argue that if you subtract from their premiums the amount of dividends, then the *net* cost of their product will be less.

Dividends may be taken in cash. They may also be

applied toward the payment of premiums. They may be accumulated with interest. This interest is taxable. Finally, the dividends may be employed to buy paid-up insurance. This option involves no physical examination and is usually the most efficient use of dividends.

The net premiums charged by a really good mutual company, after deducting the dividend, are frequently less than the fixed premiums charged by a stock company. On the other hand, the stock companies argue that dividends are speculative and by no means guaranteed. Dividends, say the stock companies, may diminish or disappear if investments go bad or there are epidemics which boost mortality materially. Also they say that if you invest the initial difference in cost, these investments will make up or exceed the eventual savings on participating policies. Sometimes this is true and sometimes not. It depends on whether your investment skills are better or worse than those of the insurance company. Here is a matter of choice. You must make the best comparison you can between policies you are considering. We make the suggestion that you evaluate your insurance adviser by asking for as much data as possible on comparative costs, and other available criteria (see chapter 14).

GROUP INSURANCE AND ANNUITIES

As touched on earlier, many large companies offer group life insurance. The classic example of group life is the insurance of large groups of employees. Sometimes, if the group is large enough, the group consists of all the employees of a single company. Sometimes it encompasses all the employees of companies or governmental units (such as all the employees of New York City or of the fire department of Los Angeles). Sometimes it includes all the members of a lodge, such as the Elks or of a professional organization such as the New York State Bar Association. At times it includes all people in a special situation, such as persons who take out mortgage loans from a savings institution or insurance company and elect to have the amount of the mortgage debt covered, should they die before the mortgage is paid off.

In most cases the insurance is issued without medical examination. However, when the group is not large enough, or if the amount of insurance on the lives of some of the participants is unusually large, then the insurance company will insist upon either a medical examination by a physician or in some cases at least filling out a questionnaire about the medical experience of the applicant. The latter will ask about specific illnesses of the applicant or of her mother or father. For example, some companies will not issue a large policy, either group or individual, if either parent had diabetes; also, if the applicant has high blood pressure and the like.

The larger the group the easier to get full coverage. But the insurance company requires that a high percentage of the eligibles join; otherwise, most of the participants would consist of persons who couldn't get regular individual policies. In some cases, especially with a very large number of employees, the premium varies from year to year and is based on the actual experience. In such cases, the insurance companies return to the employer all premiums not actually expended in meeting death claims. This is subject to the insurance company's also retaining enough of the premiums to cover its administrative expenses plus a moderate profit.

When the group consists of employees, the coverage equals usually two, three, or four years' salary (i.e. benefits to be received).

Usually the employer pays all, or most, of the premium. The employees are called on to pay a portion of the premium in some instances, but the amount thus contributed is usually very small. Usually this contribution is averaged out between ages, with every employee contributing the same amount per $1,000 of coverage. Thus, the younger employees help carry the older ones.

When the participants are employees, the premium paid is tax deductible by the employer. (Thus the premium on a self-employed individual or a partner is not tax deductible.)

Also, the premium paid by the employer is tax deductible to the employer but is *not* taxed to the employee as extra compensation. There is one important exception to this. The cost of coverage in excess of $50,000 is taxed to the employee as added compensation. The amount of such taxable income is measured by the pure term cost of such excess over $50,000 coverage. This amount is not averaged among employees of different ages and increases sharply with increasing age. Thus the taxable rate between about age fifty-five and sixty increases almost 100 percent. Thus the tax cost increases frequently when you can least afford it. This "Table I Cost," as it is termed, is not applicable if the group life coverage is continued after retirement and termination of employment. As we shall see, this rarely occurs.

There are two major defects in group insurance.

The first of these problems is that since group life is term insurance it is temporary. If an employee terminates her employment or is fired or retires, the insurance is lost, just when it might become most necessary. A few companies continue group coverage after retirement, but in sharply reduced amounts.

As we have pointed out earlier, it is possible to convert your group policy to a permanent, individually owned policy upon termination of employment or retirement. But such conversion must be at the premiums in effect for your age at the time of conversion, not the rate in effect when the insurance first went into effect.

This makes for a much higher cost in later years. When the conversion becomes important because of such retirement or other termination, the increased burden of a new and larger expense comes at a time when it can be least afforded, yet when it is most needed. Such conversions are relatively rare. It should be remembered that with almost every insurance carrier, the group life cannot be continued into the seventies, even if the employer desires it.

The second problem with group life is that the aggregate cost over a working lifetime is usually greater than with permanent individual policies. This is particularly so if the coverage is in excess of $50,000 or if the insured could have been covered at an age below the fifties or in high income-tax brackets.

It is for these reasons that it is recommended that such insurance be supplemented by an individual policy program as soon as possible. Especially since the group coverage is usually less than the amount of insurance needed.

Comparative cost analyses can be made in individual cases by the insurance agent, and extensive studies have been made by the American Management Counsel of Weston, Connecticut.

A variant of group life insurance has recently developed. It is called "group-ordinary." Here, regular group life is combined with ordinary, that is, permanent life insurance. The employer pays for the group coverage and the employee pays for the permanent coverage. The latter carries cash values, and this portion may be, in part, paid for on the minimum-deposit basis by borrowing the cash value. This type of insurance need not be offered to all employees but may be relatively superimposed on existing group life. The Internal Revenue Service has acted in different ways about group-ordinary and has changed its ruling several times on this procedure. Accordingly, it is best to check out a proposal for this type of coverage with your tax adviser, particularly if you are a corporate executive. Also, it is advisable to check out superimposed group life insurance if you are a corporate executive.

With this type of procedure we start with regular

group life for all or most of the employees. Onto this insurance there is added additional insurance for selected groups of employees, such as the executives of a corporation.

The regular group life may, for example, give to the beneficiaries of each employee an amount of life insurance equal to two years' wages or salaries. Then the superimposed group might provide an additional three years' salary for a select group of employees. If you are an executive of a corporation, it may well be worth exploring this type of added insurance protection and compare it with other types of special employee coverage such as the type we shall now review.

MINIMUM DEPOSIT INSURANCE

For those in higher tax brackets there is an attractive way of purchasing life insurance particularly if the policy is bought in earlier years. This method is called "minimum deposit."

With few exceptions (later detailed) the premium cost is not tax deductible. With this program, premiums are usually borrowed in three out of the first seven years (to conform to tax limitations). After these seven years, the entire remaining cash value is available for borrowing. Usually by the eighth year, it is possible to recapture between 80 to 90 percent of the premiums paid. If the policy is taken before age forty-five, in the best companies, it is eventually possible to borrow the total of all premiums paid. The loan involves no personal liability. The loan is repaid either when the policy is surrendered or when it is paid at death. Recently, the interest rate (guaranteed in the policy contract) was increased from 5 to 8 percent. However, this increased interest rate on new policies is expected to enhance company earnings and thus increase dividends or decrease premiums.

What happens is that the insurance company puts the borrowed premiums to work earning investment income. Currently, such income rate may approach or even exceed the interest rate charged on premium loans. Such interest is tax deductible. The income earned by the company is reflected in tax-free insurance proceeds and tax-free dividends. What goes in is tax deductible. What comes out is tax exempt.

If your taxable income is over $30,000, or if you are under forty-five, have your insurance agent work out a schedule for you which reflects what your costs will be (after allowing for the tax deduction) on this minimum-deposit basis.

SPLIT DOLLAR INSURANCE

In this program permanent ordinary life insurance is usually used. The employer may pay a portion of the premium equal to the annual increase in cash value and the employee pays the balance. The employer owns and is beneficiary of the policy in amounts equal to its premium payments.

Alternatively, the employer may pay the entire premium and be beneficiary of the policy in amounts equal to its aggregate premium payments.

The employee is subject to tax on only a relatively small portion of the premium paid by the employer. This taxable portion is called the "PS 58 cost." It is measured by subtracting from the face amount of insurance an amount equal to the payment which the employer would receive at the death of the insured. The remainder is multiplied by the pure term rate. This result is the PS 58 cost and is taxable as earned income to the employee. Let us illustrate. Suppose a face amount of insurance is $100,000. The employer has paid aggregate premiums of $20,000 and is beneficiary of the policy to that extent at the current age of the insured, and the pure term rate is, let us say, $20 per $1,000. We subtract the employer's share of $20,000 from the total coverage of $100,000. This leaves $80,000. We multiply this by the supposed term rate of $20 per $1,000. The result is that the employee is deemed to have received extra compensation of $1,600 ($80 X $20) and is taxed on this. The result is very low-cost insurance.

Sometimes the employer gives the employee a bonus equal to the PS 58 cost and the employee contributes it back to the company as the employee's share of the cost. The advantage of this is that the employee may deduct the bonus and the employee is taxed on the same amount anyway.

There are many variants of split dollar insurance. It may be not necessarily by an employer for an employee but by one family member for another family member (or a trust for the benefit of family members).

Another variant is one used by the General Electric Company. Here, there are two sets of policies. The first set is on the officers of the corporation for the benefit of their families on a split-dollar basis. The second is key man insurance. This is insurance on executives paid for by the corporation, owned by and payable to the corporation. This coverage may be paid for on a minimum-deposit basis through borrowing the cash value.

When the insured dies, the family receives the net proceeds of the first set of policies. This is the split-dollar policy. The second policy, the key man policy, is paid to the employer (in this case the General Electric Company).

These proceeds are enough to repay to the company the premiums paid on both sets of policies plus an additional amount for the use of the company's money. This latter amount reimburses General Electric for the interest which could have been made on the money used for paying the premiums on both sets of policies.

What has happened is that the General Electric officers get insurance protection *at no ultimate cost to GE.*

This is announced in the GE proxy and in other documents which explain the program. It is a splendid way of providing maximum insurance for corporate employees at minimum cost.

This is quoted from the GE proxy notice of 1976 Statutory Meeting of Share Owners, as follows:

> Officers, division general managers, and deputy division general managers of the Company have the opportunity, subject to medical examination, to purchase additional life insurance coverage (supplementing the coverage available under the company's group insurance plans) on a basis under which the Company participates in the payment of premiums and the receipt of policy proceeds. Messrs. Jones, Dance, Parker, Weiss and 78 other Company executives participated in the program in 1975. The program is designed so that if assumptions as to mortality experience, policy dividends and other factors are realized, the Company will recover all its payments plus a factor for the use of the Company's money.

KEY MAN INSURANCE

This term refers to insurance on the life of a corporate executive or stockholder, or on the life of a partner.

Such insurance may have several purposes. It may be intended to reimburse the corporation or partnership for the loss of the services of a key executive or partner when such an individual dies. The gap left behind can be extremely costly and devastating particularly to a small, closely held corporation.

Alternatively, the purpose of such insurance may be to purchase from the estate of a deceased stockholder or partner the interest of the deceased person in the corporation or partnership. This serves several important purposes. In the first place, it can substitute cash for an interest in a business which might not be salable at all, or salable at a disastrous discount. Also, it can help the survivors avoid the problem of dealing with an estate where the executor (who has the responsibility for collecting the assets of a deceased person) or the executor's attorney may know little or nothing about the business. Such an involvement of an estate can be disastrous for all parties. Also, if the estate is not bound to sell to the survivors, it may sell to a stranger who may interfere with the successful management of the business.

One of the most important federal courts—the Circuit Court of Appeals (second in importance only to the U. S. Supreme Court)—said in its opinion on a tax case involving a company known as the Emeloid Company, as follows:

> What corporate purpose could be considered more essential than key man insurance? The business that insures its buildings and machinery and automobiles from every possible hazard can hardly be expected to exercise less care in protecting itself against the loss of two of its most vital assets— managerial skill and experience. In fact the government has not seriously contended here that key man insurance is not a proper corporate purpose.

> We need not, however, rest this decision on the state of the record in the absence of the trust agreement, as it is not in the least inconsistent with the purpose originally underlying the purchase of the insurance. The trust was designed to implement that original purpose, and, at the same time, add a further business objective, viz., to provide for continuity of harmonious management. Harmony is the essential catalyst for achieving good management; and good management is the sine qua non of long-term business success. Petitioner, deeming its management sound and harmonious, conceived of the trust to insure its con-

tinuation. Petitioner apparently anticipated that, should one of its key stockholder-officers die, those beneficially interested in his estate might enter into active participation in corporate affairs and possibly introduce an element of friction. Or his estate, not being bound by contract to sell the stock to petitioner, might sell it to adverse interests. The fragile bark of a small business can be wrecked on just such uncharted shoals.

There are several tax considerations which should be kept in mind. It is important in small corporations or partnerships to have what is known as a buy-sell agreement among the principals. This can be helpful in several important ways. It provides *in advance* for a means of fixing the price of the deceased person's interest in the business. This avoids bitter and expensive arguments about a fair price for the interest in the business. Also, if properly drawn by a competent attorney, such an agreement is binding on the government in determining the price at which the interest will be taxed to the estate of the owner. Thus, the buy-sell agreement can control the amount of tax but also provide the cash to pay the tax.

Another tax consideration relates to the ownership of the insurance. Usually, key man insurance is owned by the corporation whose stock is being purchased. Where the purpose of the corporation is to use the proceeds in connection with a buy-sell agreement, it can save a tax between 25 and 70 percent of the insurance proceeds by having the insurance owned not by the corporation, but by the insured's fellow stockholders (or by trusts for the benefit of their families). The reason for this is that once the insurance proceeds get into the corporation coffers, there will be a heavy tax involved in getting it from the corporation into the hands of the surviving shareholders. This tax can be avoided by a cross-insurance program between the individual shareholder and partners or their family trusts.

A further purpose of key man insurance is to provide resources to a corporation or partnership with which to continue paying compensation to the family of a deceased stockholder for a period of years. Such insurance may be self-financing, as stated by the explanation by General Electric with regard to its own key man insurance on its officers.

SPECIAL POLICY PROVISION

With regard to any policy of life insurance, both new and old, you should review with your insurance agent the optional provisions that you may want to include in the policy.

One of these provisions, mentioned earlier, is called "automatic premium loan." There may come a time when, because of illness or a long trip or the like, you may neglect to pay a premium, either when due or within the thirty-day "grace period." At the end of the grace period, if the current premium is not paid, the insurance company will take the cash value and buy paid-up insurance to the extent available with the cash value. This is usually quite limited. However, if you have the automatic premium loan provision, the insurance company will take your cash value and use it to pay the premium due to keep the policy alive until you can resume paying the premiums in cash.

Another very important option which should be exercised when the policy is originally issued, should you so desire, is the "disability waiver" provision. This means that if the insured becomes disabled from earning a living, the further payment premiums will be waived, and they will be paid by the insurance company instead. This means that not only will the policy be kept alive, but that its cash value will keep increasing. As you know, the cash value can be borrowed to tide over emergency expenses. While this provision requires a small extra premium, many people find it worthwhile to have this extra provision.

Another provision you may want is the one that will double the amount of insurance in case of accidental death of the insured. This is called the "double indemnity" provision. Since accidents are a major cause of premature death, this sometimes becomes a useful benefit. However, the cost of this provision should be compared with a straight accident policy. This is discussed in the chapter on casualty insurance.

There are all kinds of other options which may be offered by insurance companies, and you should have your insurance agent explain them all to you before you select your insurance policy.

RATED POLICIES

If a prospective insured is not in good health, the insurance company will be willing to issue the policy only if an extra additional premium is paid. This is called a "rated policy." Policies may also be rated if the proposed insured is in a hazardous occupation.

People frequently become angry when told that they have been rated. Instead of responding in this fashion, you should take thought as to whether the rating doesn't increase your need for insurance protection. Usually the best thing to do is to arrange if you can for the removal or reduction of the rating if the condition is improved or eliminated. If you are overweight or have high blood pressure (frequent cause for rating) you should determine whether the insurance company will eliminate the rating if, for a significant period of time, the weight or blood pressure are at appropriate levels. In several instances where persons had neglected their health, the rating served the essential purpose of scaring them into seeking medical assistance in a fashion which probably saved them from premature death.

PAYMENT OPTIONS

If an insured dies and you are the beneficiary of the insurance you have several choices as to how you will receive payment of the proceeds.

You can take these proceeds in a single, lump sum and invest them in securities, with a savings institution, or in the purchase of a home, or other income producing property. You may also use the proceeds to pay off the mortgage on your home. However, if the mortgage has been in effect for some time, you should check whether the interest you have to pay is not less than the income you might earn from some other investment.

Another choice is to leave the money with the insurance company and receive interest from the insurance company.

A third choice is to receive payment in installments, for example ten annual installments with interest on the unpaid balance.

A final choice is an annuity settlement. This is an arrangement whereby the insurance company calculates your life expectancy from its statistical data (usually with amazing accuracy). It then calculates the payment of the principal plus interest over this period. This is your annuity. If you die prematurely the annuity stops and you and your family are the losers. If you live to 110, the insurance company will have to keep paying. Statistics establish that people receiving annuities tend to live longer than the general population. It concluded that the peace of mind resulting from assured income accounts for this. But with inflation as it is, this security is not as reliable as it used to be. Some insurance companies increase the annuity as their earnings increase (see prior section on mutual companies). Other means of combating inflation, such as putting all or part of the insurance proceeds in the stock market and having the payments vary with the investment results, have, on the whole, had dismal results. However, when you come to collect insurance, you might well check out what inflation hedges via "variable annuities" may then have become available and what their records have been.

The above comments about annuities have been about "pure" annuities where payments continue as short or as long as the life of the annuitant, be it long or short. But this "bet" can be hedged. For example, you may elect a "life annuity, ten years certain." This means that if the annuitant lives for less than ten years the payment will continue for the balance of the ten years certain. If the annuitant, for example, lives only four years, the payments will continue to her family for six years more, until payments have been made for a total of ten years. You may also elect twenty years certain. Another choice is to have a guarantee that at least the principal amount of the insurance will be paid, no matter how long the annuitant lives. Of course, this means that the interest on the principal will have been lost, since only the principal repayment is guaranteed.

In a recent situation, a woman of about sixty lost her husband and had one policy paying about $150,000. She, after much thought, concluded that a lifetime annuity which would provide income as long as she might live was the safest choice. However, when she discovered that a guarantee that the annuity would continue for *at least ten years* would reduce her monthly income by only fifteen dollars, she decided to take the life annuity, ten year certain option.

If you are faced with such a choice it may be good to check with a physician and review your family longevity situation as well as the needs of your family for income, before making a decision.

In any case this decision as to which option to exercise will be one of the most important decisions in your life and should not be made impulsively.

How to Choose Your Insurance Company and Select the Best Policy

One of the most difficult things in financial planning is to make a comparison between life insurance companies and between specific policies. Even sophisticated financial officers of large corporations frequently become confused in this respect.

As we pointed out before in comparing term insurance with permanent insurance, term insurance is cheaper than permanent insurance in the earlier years but over a period of time, could become much more expensive. This does not mean that term insurance should never be purchased. It does mean that raw figures cannot be compared without thought as to the purpose of the insurance being purchased and the period of time during which it will be held.

Even within specific types of insurance there are large variations. Some policies have a certain net cost the first five or ten years of their existence, and a different comparative cost on a twenty-year period or over a projected lifetime.

As explained before, dividends paid on insurance policies by mutual life companies or by stock companies with "participating policies" can be critically important in a comparison of net cost. Yet, no company will guarantee dividends. It is thus generally wise, *among other approaches*, to take the previously projected dividends actually paid. In some cases these dividends will be less than those projected; in others, they might be a good deal more. But even then there may be special considerations which involve dividends. For example, for some years prior to January 1, 1978, insurance companies issuing policies in New York State had to make loans on cash values at an interest rate no higher than 5 percent. In other states the rate could be from 6 to 8 percent (but since January 1, 1978, this same rule applies in New York State because of legislation enacted in 1977). Because of the lower interest rate, some companies had a lower scale of dividends on their New York policies than on their policies issued elsewhere. Other companies had a uniform dividend scale. With the increase of interest rates on New York policies, it will be interesting to note what effect this will have had on dividend rates on mutual policies issued in New York.

Also, the relation of guaranteed cash values (together with the cash values based on the use of dividends for paid-up additions) is a factor to be considered.

Most companies base the age of the insured (on which the premium cost will be calculated) on his or her age at the closest birthday; others base it on age at the preceding birthday. Accordingly, when a prospective insured is more than six months from his or her last birthday, it is important to know how age is calculated. Again, this does not mean that the company that figures age to the preceding birthday is necessarily the cheaper in net cost. This is just one factor to be examined with many others.

Many comparisons are made by subtracting from the total of premiums paid the total dividends, if any declared, and the cash surrender value after a period of time, such as twenty years. This is not necessarily meaningful because over a twenty-year period the net cost may be higher or less than during the first ten years. You have to make an allowance, just as the General Electric Company (quoted above) made for the "use of the money." This means that the premiums paid to an insurance company could, theoretically, have been invested in income-producing property elsewhere. This is by no means to say that in a given situation the payment of premiums is the best possible investment a person could make. Frequently, it is. But insurance companies and their policies should be compared, not only with each other, but with other uses of your money. In addition to the foregoing there are many other factors, such as the availability of options, the strictness of the underwriting, whether one company will "rate" (as above) a prospective insured who is not in perfect health, and many other factors.

This presents a hopeless task for the layperson, however sophisticated. The thing to do is to engage an agent in whom you have confidence and let him advise you.

But how do you select the right agent? Just as you would select an attorney, accountant, a physician, or an architect. You make inquiries from people whose judgment you trust and then you ask the recommended agent for other references, preferably from people with whom he or she has done business for many years.

It is then important to evaluate the work of the agent by seeing whether he or she is too simplistic, on the one hand, or overwhelms you with material too detailed for you to understand, on the other hand.

In any and all events, it is important to realize that the selection of an insurance agent and insurance company and an insurance policy is one of the most important financial choices you will make during your entire lifetime (see chapter 14).

Some agents give legal advice as part of their job. This frequently may be mistaken. For example, many agents recommend that a policy should be turned over to the wife of the insured. This is usually poor advice. In many cases a husband's group or personal life insurance policy should either be assigned to you (and not just make you the beneficiary), better yet (from a tax point of view), the insurance should be put into an irrevocable trust for you and any children you may have. The reason for assigning the insurance is that if the person whose life is insured has any ownership rights with regard to the insurance, the amount is includible in determining the size of the taxable estate of the insured. This can be avoided by assigning the insurance to the beneficiary. It can also be avoided if the insurance is part of a qualified pension or profit-sharing trust. If assigned to a wife her estate will have to pay a tax on any part of the insurance not spent by the widow during her life. However, if assigned to a trust for the benefit of the widow and the children of the insured, the proceeds can be used for the benefit of the widow and children and not taxed in her estate at her death. Consequently, you should look for an insurance agent who will cooperate with your tax adviser; and an attorney and accountant who will recommend you to a specialist in this area (see chapter 14).

One thing is certain if you are employed by a corporation, particularly a large corporation. Any agent who develops a program for you without reviewing in detail the insurance coverage given to you by your company is not doing his job well.

INCONTESTABILITY

It is very important to state facts very carefully in making out the application for insurance. If you do not, you may find yourself without insurance and your heirs may be getting back just the premiums paid, instead of the policy amount of insurance. This will be the case if your application incorporates a material misstatement of fact. In most instances policies become "incontestable" after a period of one or two years after the date of issuance. Since, fairly frequently, with best intentions, mistakes of fact are made on the insurance application, it is important to know that in most instances, policies become "incontestable" after a period of one or two years after date of issuance. But check the laws of your state. Always drop an insurance agent who suggests misrepresentation or concealment in making out an application.

TAX ASPECTS OF INSURANCE

The proceeds of insurance, in almost every case, are substantially greater than the amount of premiums paid. This profit is usually free from income or capital gains taxes. This is one of the greatest advantages to insurance as an investment medium. This immunity can be lost, however, if you *sell* the policy. There are some highly technical exceptions to this rule which are too complex for present enumeration. If you are going to transfer a policy or have one transferred to you, make sure you check with your own tax adviser as to whether the transfer is under circumstances which will make the net proceeds taxable.

Generally speaking, premiums paid for insurance are not tax deductible. There are some exceptions to this rule. If group insurance is purchased, the premium paid by the employer is tax deductible. But part of this premium, as explained above, which pays for insurance benefits in excess of $50,000, is tax deductible to the employee.

Also, if insurance is purchased as part of a pension or profit-sharing plan, the premium is deductible by the employer as part of the contributions to a qualified plan. Again a small portion of this premium is taxable to the employee.

To a substantial extent, deductibility can be achieved by borrowing out the cash value of the policy and using it to pay the premiums; and then deducting the interest paid on the loan. This is an extremely complicated procedure which is useful only to people in a high tax bracket, but it is certainly worth examining.

If a policy is given away, it is a taxable gift to the extent of the "terminal reserve" (almost exactly equal to the cash surrender value) less any loans already made against the cash value. Whether or not the gift will actually be taxed depends on whether it can qualify for the annual "exclusion" of $3,000 per donor and per donee (a married couple can give away $6,000 in cash or net cash value to each separate donee every year and not have it count as a taxable gift). Moreover, gifts are not subject to a gift tax until the aggregate of all gifts made (in excess of the annual exclusion mentioned before) reaches a certain amount. This amount varies from year to year. Under tax law, by 1981, gifts will only be taxed when they, in the aggregate, have amounted to approximately $175,000, after subtracting the annual exclusion.

If insurance is held in a trust, as is frequently the best way to do it, the question of whether gifts to such a trust qualify for the exclusion depends on how the trust is drawn and calls for the advice of a specially trained tax expert in each given case.

Recently, out of forty-five sophisticated persons participating in a financial seminar in Scottsdale, Arizona, forty-two were of the opinion that the proceeds of life insurance were not subject to estate tax. Only three were of the opinion that proceeds were subject to an estate tax. The three were correct. If the insured has any "incidents of ownership," the proceeds are part of his taxable estate. An incident of ownership is any real power of disposition or control over a policy, such as the power to name the beneficiary, change the beneficiary, borrow on the policy, and the like. If you attempt to get insurance out of the taxable estate of yourself or a relative, the best way to do it is to put it into a trust. This can save more taxes than almost any other procedure you will be faced with. Yet, it is of the utmost importance that the trust be drawn with the greatest of skill by a superspecialist in this field. This is one of the most difficult and important areas in the entire field of financial and tax planning. Even if the trust is so worded as to achieve estate tax immunity, it will be worse than useless if the trust is drawn in some fashion which does not accomplish the best results, financial and personal, for the members of the family whom it is intended to benefit. What would go into one of these trusts is discussed in detail in the chapter on the use of trusts as a financial-planning vehicle.

It should be borne in mind that if insurance is transferred to a trust within three years of the death of the insured donor, the proceeds are subject to inclusion in the taxable estate of the insured, in whole or in part (depending on the age of the policy at the time of transfer). Therefore, when insurance is first issued, it should be considered whether or not it should be in the name of a trust from the very beginning. Sometimes this is not feasible but it would be worthwhile to think about it in any case. Group insurance and "split dollar" insurance should generally be put into a trust.

WIFE AND CHILD INSURANCE

Most insurance purchased is on the life of a husband or father. If such insured is the main source of support of a family, this is important.

Generally, however, insurance on the life of a wife is overlooked. With close to 50 percent of our work force female, this becomes, self-evidently, unsound. Moreover, if a wife dies before a husband (which occurs in approximately one-third of all marriages) the husband will find himself paying heavier income taxes because of an inability to use joint returns; and higher estate taxes because of loss of a "marital deduction." Another very important factor is that insurance on women is considerably cheaper than insurance on *men,* usually, because insurance on a woman is not more than the cost of insurance on a man approximately *three years younger* than the woman.

Another factor to be considered is that most men of fairly substantial means, or of great wealth, bequeath half of their estate to the spouse and thus avoid paying estate taxes on that half. Also, in the western and southern "community property" states, the wife owns half of what the husband acquired through earnings during the period of the marriage. In addition to this, if property is held jointly and the wife dies before the husband, the husband generally will have to pay tax on the entire value of the jointly held property.

Accordingly, it is important to explore with a skilled insurance agent and other financial advisers, whether a person has gotten to the point in life where insurance on the life of a wife should be purchased.

Insurance on the life of a child can be very useful, especially at younger ages when the insurance cost is so relatively minuscule that the premiums paid are to be deemed primarily savings. Where a family has a daughter married to some young man, one of the least costly and successful means of providing for the security of the daughter is to give both the daughter and son-in-law annual gifts for the purpose of buying insurance on the life of the son-in-law. If both parents are alive, these gifts may aggregate as high as $12,000 a year for each of the daughters. The father can give up to $3,000 to his daughter and a similar amount to his son-in-law. The wife can give a similar amount. Of course, a smaller amount can be paid and should be considered. If the proceeds are invested in insurance on the life of the son-in-law, after a very few years, the increase in cash value can be enough to keep the policy alive without further gifts; although bequests from the parents to pay such premiums can be even more useful. While loans to pay premiums will decrease the amount of insurance available on the death of the son-in-law, it also follows that a lesser sum of money *can buy an equal amount of annual support for the daughter*. As the net insurance shrinks, the cost of an annuity shrinks at almost the same rate. This is one of the best ways for parents or grandparents to insure the financial security of their married daughters or granddaughters.

GENERAL CONCLUSION

From the length of this chapter, it can be correctly inferred that this area of thinking is not only one of the most important, but one of the most complex in the entire field of financial planning. We strongly recommend that this chapter be reread several times; then a competent life insurance agent be selected to review the chapter with the reader and apply it to existing insurance privately held or employer-supplied together with the recommended additional insurance. This project, above all, should be a family affair, encompassing all family members sufficiently experienced to grasp this subject.

8

Protecting It: Health and Casualty Insurance

DISABILITY INCOME INSURANCE

Disability income insurance receives less attention proportionately to its importance than almost any other financial program. As a matter of fact, disability insurance is sometimes more important than life insurance. Life insurance *can* have added disability provisions under which the insurance company waives further premiums if the insured becomes disabled, and in that case may also pay an income to him.

Disability insurance can be more necessary than life insurance because when a person dies, expenses cease, except for the last illness expense and the administration of his estate. Moreover, the widow frequently can go out and get a job. But if a head of household becomes disabled, not only does the income cease, but expenses expand—because the disabled person has to be taken care of (usually by the wife, who has to stay home to do it).

An actuarial group accumulated some statistics in 1964 showing that if a man is disabled at age fifty-two for one year, there is almost a 70-percent chance that he will continue to be disabled for two years and more than a 50-percent chance that he will continue to be disabled for five years. If the disability lasts for two years there is better than a 75-percent chance that it will continue for another two years, and almost a 60-percent chance that it will continue for another five years. These percentages vary, of course, but they do emphasize the seriousness of the situation.

Here is another advantage of disability income insurance. Within certain technical limitations the cost of such insurance is deductible either by the insured or by the employer. Also, the insurance, within another set of limitations, is free of tax to the recipient. If a man in the 35-percent tax bracket received $100 a week of disability income, this equals $666 of taxed monthly salary. If he is in the 50-percent bracket, it is the equivalent of $866 of monthly salary. In addition the employer is saved from the unpleasant dilemma of either paying a disabled employee a continuing salary or becoming known as an employer who does not treat employees fairly.

Disability income insurance contracts have more loopholes than probably any other type of insurance, however, and such a contract should be studied for you by an expert. Your regular agent may be good at life insurance but may know very little about disability insurance. Even though your disability insurance is furnished to you free of cost by your employer, it will pay you to have it analyzed by an expert. It will be worth the fee. The loopholes revealed may be unavoidable, but it is better to know that they exist. Here are some of the more common loopholes:

The policy may not provide for an automatic premium loan.

It may not have a provision for waiver of premium during disability.

It may exclude disability occurring in a war zone or from military causes.

At times there is a delay before the disability income commences—in some cases up to six months. At times there is a delay that varies with the kind of disability. Find out when it is payable.

Certain disabilities are sometimes completely excluded, for instance those resulting from mental disorders. Beware of this. 25 percent of all hospital beds in the U. S. are occupied by the mentally disturbed.

Incontestable policy clauses vary; sometimes policies are incontestable for any reason after two years have passed. In other cases they are incontestable only where there are mistakes in the application—but not if there is a willful misrepresentation.

Some policies state that only conditions occurring after the policy goes into effect are covered. Others specify that after two years any physical disorders are deemed to have originated after the policy existed and cannot be contested.

The amount of disability income sometimes varies or the employee's other policies eliminate such variations.

There are some policies that pay only for total disability or pay in the case of partial disability only as a result of an accident—not a result of an illness. In other cases, partial disability will be covered only if it follows a period of complete disability.

Sometimes delayed disability is not covered. Sometimes an accident, especially in head injury cases, does not disable a person for a long time after the accident occurs. Some policies exclude coverage unless the disability occurs within a fixed time after the accident.

In some instances, a policy reserves the right to pay the insured a lump sum instead of monthly or weekly payments. This could constitute a serious loss.

In some cases, a policy stops benefits when there is a partial recovery and when the insured is able to return to some kind of work, albeit at a lower income. With some contracts he loses his benefits, with others the benefits continue, at least in part.

Some contracts provide very limited coverage for recurring disability. As an example, a policy may provide for payments for five years or for a year on any given disability. The insured may be disabled for nine months, recover for six months, and then become disabled from the same illness. Under this kind of circumstance if a contract carries a one-year limitation the recurrence would be treated as one disability and the insured would be entitled to only three months' more disability, giving the insured a full year of coverage only.

The best coverage, of course, is one that continues for life, and it may be worth the extra expense. Other policies continue to age sixty-five on the supposition that the insured will then receive a pension or social security, or both. Still other policies continue to age sixty-five and are then converted into an endowment policy providing an annuity. When this is combined with a provision waiving premiums during disability, the endowment income may be as great as the disability income. This kind of provision, as a rule, is found only in disability clauses attached to life insurance.

It is of the utmost importance to consider paying a slightly larger premium for what is known as "disability waiver." This means that if you become wholly and permanently disabled, the insurance company will keep on paying the premiums on your life insurance policy. Not only will this keep the death protection going, but the cash value of the policy will continue to increase and, if it is a participating policy, or mutual company policy, it will continue to pay dividends. This means that in addition to the continuing death protection, you have a resource in the continually increasing cash value, which you can borrow, and dividends, which you can spend. This provides excellent security in the case of disability.

It is extremely tricky to define disability. It is sometimes defined in terms that treat a person as disabled if his income is reduced by 75 percent as a result of the disability for a period of time. Another definition describes disability as the inability to perform one's regular work. Some are more stringent and require that the owner be unable to be gainfully employed, not only in his regular work, but in any type of work for which he is prepared by experience, education, or training. Therefore, a secretary whose eyesight was injured and who could no longer be a secretary might be disqualified because she could become a telephone operator. Even worse is the definition that excludes disability if the insured can engage in *any* gainful occupation regardless of whether or not it fits in with his or her training or experience.

One very tricky clause requires that disability be independent of any other causes. This provision combined with one that rules out conditions in existence when the insurance went into effect can be limiting. For example, someone who had very bad eyesight and fell as a result of it might arguably be denied coverage for the disability resulting from the fall.

The worst drawback to some disability insurance is the power of the company either to cancel it or to refuse to renew it. This means that you may pay premiums for years only to have your policy canceled the minute you have one accident or severe illness—or when you reach a certain age. If you can afford it, be sure you get noncancelable lifetime insurance, or at least insurance that continues until a pension commences.

It's impossible to generalize a formula for the optimum combination of low-cost and effective coverage. Circumstances vary with the state of health of the insured, sex, age, income, and type of work. However, you can begin to make an estimate of the effectiveness of your coverage if you have the above loopholes in mind.

Of course when the wage earner is disabled the situation is serious, but it can also be bad when a housewife is disabled. Oftentimes the family then needs a housekeeper, at least on a part-time basis. While medical and surgical insurance can and should cover all the members of an entire family, it is very difficult to obtain an insurance policy on an unemployed wife (a homemaker is considered "unemployed") that will pay the family enough to hire a housekeeper in case she becomes disabled. The reason for this is that traditionally disability income insurance provides weekly or monthly income based on the earnings of the insured. Since housewives do not have earnings, they are usually not eligible for disability insurance. This is absurd, since a housewife has at least as much economic value as a woman employed in a factory, and frequently more. At long last some insurance companies are beginning to write insurance on housewives. This coverage should be obtained if at all possible.

MEDICAL AND SURGICAL INSURANCE

Nothing can bankrupt a family faster than illness or an accident. Medical, surgical, and hospital costs are increasing all along. And investment programs supplying this kind of assistance with medical, dental, surgical, psychiatric, or hospital care are usually entirely inadequate. Therefore, it is most important that such protection be provided either by the employer or by the employee himself. Employer-provided insurance could be an important consideration in choice of jobs and usually requires some supplementary, individually purchased insurance.

Such insurance is Blue Cross (medical) and Blue Shield (surgical), accident and health insurance, or Major Medical insurance. Whether supplied by the employer or privately acquired, all such insurance should be checked for loopholes, which usually parallel the exclusions, exceptions, and limitations mentioned above with regard to disability income insurance. The difference between these insurance policies and disability income insurance is that the latter, as its name implies, pays the beneficiary when disabled and unable to earn a living, and the other types of insurance pay all or part of the bills for doctors, dentists, surgeons, psychiatrists, or hospitals.

We cannot begin to enumerate all of the loopholes that should be checked. Be sure to check those mentioned in connection with disability insurance, and also others. It pays to have an insurance adviser review your own policy and/or your employer's policy and amend the limitations. Limitations may be found that are not mentioned in this chapter, but if the adviser fails to allude to those we do mention, you would be well advised to get another expert.

Deductibility provisions in these types of insurance are one special consideration. Some do not cover the first $50 or $100 of bills. This tends to discourage the insured from running to a doctor or hospital at each little ache or pain; the administrative costs are disproportionately high on small claims. On the other hand, the very fact that a person is discouraged from seeking frequent medical or surgical assistance could cause a much more serious illness to result. Morever, these deductible features add up to pretty sizable amounts in the average family.

Remember to check if the policy covers dental treatment and whether or not it covers the cost of medical treatment at home or only in the doctor's office, or only in the hospital. One of your authors had a minor operation that took about fifteen minutes under local anesthetic; it was intended to help a "tennis elbow." He had to pay the total bill of $300 because he made the mistake of having it done in the surgeon's office. If he had entered a hospital and stayed overnight he would have been covered by his insurance.

Another example concerns a friend of ours who feared that one of his children might need psychiatric hospitalization. One of his friends, an employee of a large corporation, had been the beneficiary of a group policy that provided compensation for psychiatric hospitalization. His friend's daughter developed severe psychiatric problems requiring hospitalization that cost

$1,500 a month. His company's group Major Medical policy covered this and he was saved $18,000. Our friend, who was the head of a small service organization employing only eight people, sought similar coverage. He was particularly anxious to obtain this because, within certain limits, medical insurance costs are tax deductible and benefits are tax free. However, he was told that his group was too small to permit group coverage and that coverage under an individual policy was so limited in amount as not to represent signicant protection.

Two years later he actually found himself faced with the choice between putting his child in a state institution (at the very time it was being investigated for alleged brutality in its psychiatric ward) or spending about $1,500 a month. He felt he had no choice but to bring himself to the verge of bankruptcy by placing his child in a private institution. A month later he found that a major insurance company, *with which his own organization was working,* had installed some months before his child's illness manifested itself what was called a mini-group plan for groups as small as four people, and that his own near-bankruptcy could have been avoided and his expenditures substantially reduced had this coverage been taken. The insurance company did not tell him about it because his job was in a completely unrelated field. Remember, one out of every four hospital beds is devoted to a psychiatric patient.

His friend had been extremely lucky in working for a company that had an excellent policy. But you can't be sure you or your family members are protected against this all-too-frequent catastrophe just because you have a Major Medical policy or work for a large company that has a group Major Medical policy. Many large company policies provide little or no psychiatric care, or, if they do, limit the amount and period of coverage so stringently that they do little to ameliorate the costs of this particular calamity. In one instance a provision provides for only 50 percent of a psychiatrist's bill and for only one visit per week for one year. As of this writing any adequate coverage is difficult whether you buy it individually or are covered through a group policy. We strongly recommend that your family be regularly checked out not only medically but psychiatrically. If there are any danger signals you should at least know how much protection you have. Then, if it is not adequate, you can either endeavor to obtain the best individual coverage possible, seriously consider a job with a company that has at least reasonably adequate group coverage, or, if that is not available at least consider moving to a state that provides the best public psychiatric care. A nationally noted physician has stated that while there are no really good state institutions for the severely mentally ill, among the best are New York, Massachusetts, Illinois, Connecticut, and Pennsylvania. These institutions need more support and probably reorganization, and toward this end Massachusetts, New York, and perhaps Connecticut have accomplished something.

If work involves some particular part of the body, such as the legs of a ballet dancer or the hands of a pianist or violinist, it is usually worthwhile to carry specific insurance in this respect.

All types of insurance need reviewing annually so as to cover increased earning power, increased cost of living, and increased cost of medical and surgical care. Another hidden snare, for example, only discovered when it is too late, is that many Major Medical contracts limit coverage to $10,000 or $15,000. For a junior executive in today's economy this is a totally inadequate benefit, particularly if the limitation is on a lifetime basis. After a small number of major illnesses, protection practically ceases to exist, except if there is a new physical examination, and this probably cannot be passed if the lifetime limitation has been exhausted.

One aspect of all types of insurance other than life insurance is whether, and to what extent, they cover the family of the individual. Many policies cover the children, but only up to age eighteen. Frequently some serious accident or illness occurs three days after the eighteenth birthday. Therefore, the extent of coverage both in terms of age, relationship, and amount should be reviewed at regular intervals, both for employer-furnished insurance and privately acquired insurance.

TRAVEL INSURANCE

Travel insurance is another important field. Usually for less than $1,000 a person who does lots of flying can buy about $1,000,000 worth of insurance. Employers often provide such insurance, but it would be worth your while to have additional personal insurance because it so cheap. If this insurance would be held in a separate trust, it would be free from inheritance and estate taxation in the case of either the death of the husband or the wife. Thus, for a relatively few dollars this can be an enormous protection. Since air travel is probably the safest travel today, air insurance is very cheap. You don't need $1,000,000 worth of insurance, but a few hundred thousand costs only a few hundred dollars a year and it certainly is worthwhile.

If your general insurance broker isn't really a competent general broker who goes over all your insurance in every type of risk, you may someday find yourself in terrible straits.

Most companies provide travel insurance for their employees, but in some cases it only covers them when on company business and, in most cases, is insufficient in amount. So we advise you to carry your own travel insurance. Moreover, the corporation should carry key man life insurance and travel insurance on its executives for its own benefit. In one case a large group of executives from three different companies out on special assignment in private company planes were killed in one week through three separate company-plane crashes. All were from nationally known U.S. corporations. Two of these companies were Bechtel Corporation and Harris, Upham & Company. The loss of the third company involved was so devastating to management that it requested that its name not be divulged.

WORKMEN'S COMPENSATION INSURANCE

To employers: It is particularly important that you carry workmen's compensation insurance. An employee is entitled to receive compensation, under the law, sometimes for life, for any illness or injury connected with work. If you go into business for yourself and employ a secretary or telephone operator, you may neglect the purchase of workmen's compensation insurance. Your secretary might trip and fall while rushing to answer a telephone, break a hip, and become a semipermanent invalid. You would be obliged to pay such employee workmen's compensation for a long period of time, even though you were entirely free from neglect, and, if not covered by this insurance, it could be a crushing financial burden for you.

Our farm manager was plowed into by a car skidding into the wrong lane on an icy road while he was delivering milk. Even though the manager was totally free from negligence, since he was taking cans of milk to the dairy in the course of his work, he was entitled to workmen's compensation. This could have spelled a tremendous financial loss in the absence of insurance protection. Get a letter from your insurance broker telling you what risks are covered by your policies and what risks are not covered. If, however, the broker makes a mistake, the insurance company is not bound —so it is well to have these representations confirmed by a letter signed by an officer of the insurance company itself.

LIABILITY INSURANCE

We mention the importance of carrying adequate liability insurance in the section dealing primarily with automobile accidents. Most automobile owners carry insurance against liability for accidents, but usually not in sufficiently large amounts. However, most accidents occur in the home, or outside the home, but not in sufficiently large amounts. However, many accidents occur that are not connected with automobiles; therefore, while on the subject of general insurance, let us urge you to maintain an overall liability policy that covers you in case a guest slips on the ice in front of your doorstep or an itinerant worker falls and is paralyzed for life.

Above-mentioned insurance can be supplemented by umbrella or catastrophe insurance, which picks up liability only when damage occurs through some unexpected disaster and when it exceeds existing coverage. The cost for $5,000,000 worth of such coverage (which might be needed if your youngster plows the family jalopy into a school bus and forces it off the road and down an embankment) is relatively small and well worth checking out with your insurance broker.

In this general area of liability insurance there is a special type called professional insurance. One famous lawyer lost his entire life's savings because he did not have professional insurance. He had been a judge for many years and after his retirement returned to private practice in Brooklyn, New York. Someone asked his opinion about a legal problem under the law of another state. Usually a lawyer's opinion is just that—an opinion—and in the absence of gross negligence he may not be liable if the guess is wrong. After all, the U.S. Supreme Court often has 5–4 decisions. But this unfortunate lawyer happened to give a faulty opinion about the law of another state, and he was held liable for the very extensive damages his client suffered as a result. Professional insurance would have protected him. Professional or malpractice insurance is also advantageous for the claimant. It is useful in all types of professions that require special skills.

FIRE AND CASUALTY INSURANCE

Of course any automobile owner should carry insurance to cover the cost of car repair, no matter who is at fault. But there are other types of casualty insurance that are equally important. It's unnecessary to say that everyone should carry fire insurance on both home and its contents, office, and any similar property. There are so many types of casualty insurance that we cannot begin to deal with them all. For example, your files should be insured, and you should have adequate burglary and robbery insurance. It is very important to get a list of exclusions and exceptions in this type of insurance from a financially responsible and expert insurance broker.

There are some specific things to consider in connection with property insurance. As one example, we recently heard the fire signal of our local volunteer fire department, and a few minutes later heard the clanging bell and shrieking whistle of the fire truck quite close to our house. It was late at night, but we rushed out to investigate the scene, and a fiery one it was. Neighbors about a quarter of a mile down the road had added a new wing to their house just a few months before, and the whole new wing was burning up, apparently because of some defective electric wiring. Because of the absence of wind and the prompt action of the fire department, our neighbors were able to save the main house, but then they appraised the loss at only about 50 percent of the value of the entire structure.

A few weeks later we discovered our neighbors were most disgruntled. It seemed that when they added the new wing they had had it covered by their fire insurance policy but had not taken the advice of their fire insurance broker to increase the total coverage. After the fire they had discovered the insurance policy contained a "coinsurance" clause. This meant that if the house was not insured for its full value, the insurance company could claim that the house owner was the coinsurer

for the deficit in coverage. As it turned out, the entire
house, including the new wing had been insured for a
total of only half its value. The end result was that our
neighbors recovered only half of the loss and were out
of pocket over $10,000.

And this was only the beginning. They had put in a
claim for the loss of the contents of the new wing, and
this had been satisfied. But as we saw them week after
week in the village, it turned out that they kept remem-
bering different things that had been in the wing but
had been forgotten when they put in their claim—a
camel's-hair coat, a valuable inlaid table, and many
other items. It would seem impossible to forget important items like this, but forgotten them they had.
We must add that this forgetfulness is not only common
but almost invariable. Apparently we just cannot remember the contents of our homes. But the claim had
been put in and had been paid and satisfied; therefore,
the insurance company had been released from liability.
There was no remedy.

What our neighbors should have done was to have
had the whole house, including the new wing, appraised
by the insurance company appraisers (this is usually
done free) and obtained an adequate amount of insurance, which would have cost very little more. Then
they should have made up a list of the entire contents
of the house and had this appraised also. The list
should have been reviewed at least at annual intervals
and should have been kept in a safe deposit vault in
the local bank. Another valuable tool is to take pictures
of each room, especially your valuables, for added
proof. These pictures can be stored with your list in
the safe deposit box. Then when fire occurred, the loss
claim could have been quickly and properly prepared.
Not only would there have been no omissions because
of forgetfulness, but the value of the property would
have been established in advance. But it is essential
that these records be kept up to date and the valua-
tions refigured at regular intervals.

This sort of list must be made up in the case of death and estate probate, so it is a good idea to have it in advance in any case. A similar list is equally invaluable in a case of burglary. Since this is becoming more and more frequent, forgetfulness here would be just as bad as in the case of fire.

Also, casualty losses not covered by insurance are tax deductible subject to a $100 exclusion on nonbusiness losses. So, keep those lists and photos from before the accident and then get appraisals, repair bills, and photos *after the accident* and give them to your tax return preparer.

We can mention dozens of other loopholes. We do not suggest that these limitations are unfair, but only that it is unwise to be unaware of them. The only solution is first of all to read all policies with the greatest of care and to demand (even if it involves a fee) a detailed analysis by an insurance expert of all types of insurance affecting the lives or property of your family and a continuing review thereof.

PRODUCT LIABILITY

If a product is defective, the manufacturer or dealer may be sued for millions by thousands of users. This problem is so staggering that we can only suggest you seek the best available legal, tax and insurance advisers available. (The 1978 Law will permit—for tax years beginning after September 30, 1979—a product liability loss to be carried "back" 10 years and taxes recovered from this deduction or, the product liability loss can be carried forward against future income—all to the extent not covered by extremely expensive insurance. It also permits the special accumulation of surplus—otherwise subject to a penalty tax—for this purpose.)

9

Inheriting It

The subject of inheritance is of enormous importance to women, but they usually realize this fact only when it is too late. No one likes to discuss the subject of death, and it is emotionally upsetting to ask a parent or a spouse what their plans are in this most final of events. Yet the new federal estate tax law can result in such large estate taxes that a woman is wise to prepare herself in advance, long before she must cope.

Besides the normal distress about the subject, it is interesting to observe how much more vicious people become over inheritance than over ordinary everyday business affairs. People may be angry and upset by being cheated in a business deal, but when they find out that they are not going to get Aunt Minnie's cottage by the lake or Mom's silver tea service, they get frantic. "She always promised it to me," they cry.

WILLS

Making your will can be a painful matter. You spend a great deal of time thinking about what you should leave your husband, children, grandchildren, brothers, sisters, nieces, nephews, friends. A woman said to us recently after signing her will, "I hope everyone will be pleased, but just the same, I'm glad I won't be around to see their faces."

Some people take a shortcut and buy a printed will form at a stationery store. This is a false economy. It is better in every way to go to an attorney to have a will made for you that truly reflects your wishes and situation. Printed forms are made to cater to everyone and consequently rarely satisfy anyone. In fact, some of the provisions in the printed form may be entirely unnecessary or even harmful in your situation.

When you have gone to an attorney and made your will, do not then put it away and forget about it. Review it from time to time as your life situation changes. You grow older, your children grow older, your financial picture changes, and the tax law changes. So keep your will up to date.

Before you see an attorney, read this chapter thoroughly. It will help you in your decision making and prepare your mind in advance. For example, you will have to choose an executor or executrix. The job of the executor is to administer the will, which means to carry out the provisions contained in the will. The executor arranges to have the will probated, the assets collected, the debts and taxes paid, and then must distribute the residue either directly to the beneficiaries, or, if so provided in the will, must place the residue of the estate in a trust which then continues to hold the assets for the benefit of the trust beneficiaries.

The executors should be about your own age, or better still, younger. The reason for this is that you want them to be alive at the time of your death when the will comes into effect. If you choose old Uncle Charlie, it may be true that he is a dear and very reliable, but he is not apt to outlive you. A good executor for a husband's estate can do wonders for a bereaved woman, particularly if the executor has a competent lawyer assisting him.

An executor can be an individual, a trust company, or you can have one of each. If you have an individual and a trust company, they will be coexecutors. It is also possible in some states to name an attorney as the executor. However, this is governed by state law. In California, for example, it is not permissible to name your attorney as executor and have the attorney act in both capacities and take both an executor's commission plus legal fees for legal work on the estate.

You should also decide before you meet with your attorney who will be the beneficiaries, and what you want to leave them. Bring a list with you to the meeting, with their full names and addresses. Ask the attorney in advance what other information is required, like insurance policies or the names and addresses of charitable institutions you plan to benefit.

Quite often people have small, special bequests they want to make to special people. These may be items you change your mind about from time to time. Rather than clutter up the will with them, you should give the executor discretion with respect to tangible articles such as furniture or jewelry and then make a "List of instructions" for your family, who can generally be depended upon to carry out your wishes. However, if you are in doubt, put it in the will. These items may be things like an opal ring for your godchild, a particular oil painting for a niece, a set of encyclopedias for a nephew, or a necklace for a friend.

A beneficiary is someone to whom income or principal is distributed under a will or trust. There are "lifetime beneficiaries" and "remainder beneficiaries." A lifetime beneficiary is one who receives a bequest for life. A remainder beneficiary is one who receives the remainder of an estate after the lifetime beneficiaries have died.

As stated above, the executor may distribute the residue of the estate directly to beneficiaries or he may be required to distribute the residue to a trust which will hold the assets and pay out income to the beneficiaries. The income they receive comes from the principal of the trust. The principal is also known as the capital of the trust.

Wills should be in writing and should be witnessed and signed. It is true that in a few rare instances some states have recognized verbal wills, such as those made by soldiers in the midst of combat. A few states will recognize a holograph, which is a will made in the recognizable handwriting of the maker and does not have to be witnessed. The maker of a will is called the "testator" ("testatrix," feminine). Wills may be changed, that is, "amended by codicil." Wills may be canceled, which is the same as being "revoked."

Most states require two witnesses to a will, and others require three. The witnesses and testator or testatrix must all be present at the signing of the will, and each must see the others sign. It is usual to execute the will in the presence of an attorney. The witnesses must not only observe the signing, but must note if the testator is of sound mind and is signing of his or her own free will.

Recently a man came to our office to make his will. He was accompanied by his wife. She said as she was waiting, "I thought I'd come with him to see if I could make head or tail out of all this mumbo jumbo." It is true that the language of wills is pompous and precise to the point of being ludicrous, but the object is to be totally accurate and without double meanings. Here is an example of a "witness clause" that on first reading might have you climbing the wall. It appears above the lines where the witnesses sign.

JOHN DOE and RICHARD ROE being duly sworn on their respective oaths, depose and say that they witnessed the execution of the last will and testament of SALLY SMITH, the within named testatrix, who, in their presence, subscribed

said will at the end thereof and at the time of
making such subscription declared the instrument
so subscribed by her to be her last will and testament; that they, at the request of said testatrix
and in her sight and presence of each other, there-
upon witnessed the execution of said will by said
testatrix by subscribing thereto their names as witnesses; that said testatrix at the time of the execution of said will was in all respects competent to
make a will and not under any restraint; that they
are making this affadavit at the request of said
testatrix.

Sometime after making your will, you may wish to
make a change. This is called "amending the will." It
is done by making what is called a "codicil," and is attached to the end of your will as a part of it. For one
small change it would be troublesome and expensive to
do an entire new will. A codicil is the easiest way to
make one or two changes. Nonetheless, the codicil must
be executed with the same formalities as the will itself.

In some cases there may be such substantial changes
that it is better to start all over again and make a new
will. This is called "revoking the will." The best way
to revoke a will, that is to say, cancel it, is to make a
new one. A new will states that it cancels all previous
wills. The later date on it further supports the fact that
it supplants all prior wills. It is wise to look at your will
at least every five years to give effect to changes in your
life situation. You should also check it before moving
to a different state or country.

When a testator or testatrix dies, it is the judge of
the probate court who decides if the will is valid. (In
some states such as New York, the probate judge is
called the surrogate.) Probate court or surrogate court
is a special court, and one of its duties is to administer
wills, which is both complicated and costly.

The process of probate is started upon the death of a
testator. The heir or heirs notify their attorney who then

submits an application for probate to the probate court. It may be a month or more before the proceedings commence. During this time, a notice generally goes to the heirs and to the immediate relatives of the testator to give them an opportunity to object to the will if they suspect that it was not properly executed, or if its provisions were the result of undue influence, the absence of a sound mind, or the result of fraud or duress.

It used to be that witnesses had to come to probate court to confirm the fact that they had witnessed the execution of the will. Many states will now accept sworn statements (affidavits) attached to the will and executed by the witnesses at the time that the will itself was signed. This procedure saves a lot of time, particularly if the witnesses live far away. It should be known that the will must be probated in the state that was the official residence of the deceased at the time of death.

Only the original of a will goes to probate. However, if an original cannot be found, or has been lost, it is still possible to have a copy submitted to probate on very strong evidence that the original of the will was executed properly but then lost.

Frequently a person dies without leaving a will. This is known as "dying intestate." This can be extremely complicated, and we strongly recommend that everyone make a will, even if they have little or nothing to leave. Dying without a will means that the next of kin must go before the probate judge (or surrogate), who is obliged by law to appoint an administrator. The appointed administrator may be a person, bank, or trust company.

Many men neglect to make a will because they feel it is an invitation to death. It is up to the wife to insist that a will be made and that she be involved in planning it. This is one of the most important steps women can take in securing their emancipation. Without financial emancipation, the rest is relatively meaningless in our opinion.

A major vice of intestacy is that the state, rather than the family, decides how the estate, which the wife helped accumulate, will be divided. *And every state has its own peculiar rules.*

When the intestate estate comes under probate court regulations, it frequently involves a distribution of an estate in a fashion entirely contrary to the wishes of the deceased person and the needs of the survivor or survivors.

There are many problems of intestacy other than the frequent unfairness of intestate distribution. For one thing, the administrator of an intestate estate has to post a surety company bond, the amount of which is up to the probate court, and usually varies with the size of the estate. The object of the bond is to insure the honesty and integrity of the administrator. When there is a will the bond is usually waived if so provided in the will. Also, without a will, you do not have the prerogative of choosing your own executor. More important still, you do not have the prerogative of choosing the guardian of your minor children. This is important if the wife does not survive until the children are grown up. With a will the court is not obliged to go along with the choice of guardian but usually does. In the event that a will is out of date, the guardian named in the will may have in the meantime become an alcoholic or become otherwise undesirable, and in that case the court will use its discretion and select a more suitable guardian. But parents when they choose a guardian put a great deal of careful thought into the choice, and it is usually a good one and designed to avoid conflict as between two sides of a family. In the case of intestacy the children could end up with a guardian the parents would never have chosen.

With regard to available funds for a widow most states have what is called a "widow's allowance." To tide her over the lengthy probate proceedings, she can apply to the court for funds. In a will, the amount can be specified and may be far more generous than the amount advanced in the case of intestacy. Finally, the widow who is the beneficiary of a will, with an executor and attorney representing her, is in a far more advantageous position than the widow of a husband who has died intestate.

During the period of probate, it sometimes is advisable to initiate certain investments, but the law rigidly limits investments of money from intestate estates. The investments allowed are usually called "legals" or legal list investments and apply not only to intestate estates but to those wills that have made no provision to allow executors or trustees to invest estate assets according to their best judgment, or have made no provision for continuing a family business. "Legals" are generally low-yield bonds. When there has been no provision in a will to continue the family business, the probate court may direct that the business be sold, and this may be at a great loss if it is not a good time to make such a sale.

As stated before, a will is of critical importance. The only exception to this is when the estate is a small one and bank accounts, title to home, and other investments and household furnishings may, under the law of a particular state, be put on a joint and survivorship basis so that the estate can pass without having to go through the expense of probate, other than to have estate taxes determined and paid. This is called a "tax purposes only" probate. For this you should consult an attorney. The only hitch to this procedure is when the joint owners die in a common accident. In this case the estate is divided between the children, or if none, brothers, sisters, parents, but with all the expense of intestate proceedings.

TRUSTS

A will alone may not be enough to protect your family's fortune. There is a supplement that may be made to a will called a trust. A testamentary trust is a document or instrument used along with a will, or contained within the will, for the purpose of holding estate assets for future distribution. If the trust is independent of the will, it is called a living trust or an inter vivos trust, and the creator is called a grantor or settlor. It becomes effective on execution.

A woman may have personal or financial reasons for setting up a trust. She may have children who are too young to receive an inheritance, she may have tax problems, she may have serious doubts about the character of her son-in-law and want to protect her daughter. No one can foretell the future. One child may be a spendthrift and the other may be a financial wizard. One may be rich, another poor, one may be healthy, another may be disabled. Imperfect though trusteeship may be, a well-drawn trust administered by an independent trustee is probably as close as you can come to having your wishes carried out effectively. An independent trustee is a person who is not related to a grantor or beneficiary, or may be a corporation that is a trust company not controlled by either the grantor or any beneficiary.

Another reason for having a trust is to avoid making an outright bequest. Imagine yourself to be a woman in her early forties with three children under twelve. Should she die before her husband, it would be natural to expect him to remarry and possibly have one or two more children. She would in all likelihood want her estate to go to her husband and children and not to a second wife and subsequent children. To accomplish this she could set up a trust to provide the income of the trust to go to her husband for his life and the residue to her children when he dies. Without a trust, in most states, under the right of election law, the second wife can claim as much as one-half of his estate, or one third if there are surviving children. In some states, the surviving spouse just gets income for life; in others, the surviving spouse gets her share outright. If your husband has left you only a small part of his estate, check with an attorney other than the one who drew the will about whether you can enlarge your request by "electing against the will" to take the share you would have taken if there had been no will. This right is lost unless *promptly* exercised. In another instance, you might have a daughter-in-law you did not care for and would not want her to inherit one-third of your son's estate in the event he predeceased her. Or you might have a son-in-law who survived your daughter, and you could decide to leave your estate in trust with your surviving spouse and children as life beneficiaries, and the grandchildren as remainder beneficiaries, to exclude the son-in-law.

Trusts are essential if you want to prevent your estate from getting into the hands of a stranger or someone you dislike or distrust, rather than into the hands of more preferred heirs.

Quite apart from your principles, prejudices, or preferences, an outright bequest may have heavy tax consequences. For example, if you have wealthy relatives, or your spouse has them, and you and your spouse have substantial means as well, an outright bequest to you from a rich relative may result in a heavy estate tax in your brackets, or the income from such a bequest may increase the income tax in your brackets. It is much better for you and your family, if there are two wealthy generations, to have money bypass your generation and be used for the education of your children or grandchildren, or for other necessities.

Financing the education of children is one of the heaviest burdens with which young parents are faced today, and there are tremendous savings if you can arrange what is called a "discretionary bypass." In the case of such bypass, there may be a special tax called a "generation-skipping tax." This, however, has little application except in very large estates (more than $250,000 per child). There are means of mitigating or avoiding this extra tax. If you are wealthy enough to have the problem, you can afford skilled guidance to solve the problem.

A trust is administered by a trustee or trustees. They hold the property for the benefit of one or more individuals. A trustee may be a person or a corporation. Either one may be called an *independent* trustee. A trustee to be independent must be unrelated to the grantor or beneficiaries. If the independent trustee is a corporation, it must not be controlled by the trustee corporation. Because individual trustees may fail to survive the beneficiaries, or grow too old to handle the estate, it is advisable to have an independent corporate trustee or cotrustee. However, for various reasons the beneficiaries may at some time want to change the corporate trustee. This may not be done unless it states in the trust instrument that the beneficiaries may change the corporate trustee. One very important reason for insisting on this right is that even the best of corporate trustees will be apt to give better service if they know there is a chance that they could be changed. Many trust companies understandably dislike this provision, but an increasing number are beginning to favor it because they realize that people do not like the feeling of being locked into a situation they have no power to change. As we go on we will go into other reasons for including this power in the trust.

As stated, the testamentary trust is an actual part of the will document and because of this may be administered only in the state in which it was set up. Suppose you are the beneficiary of a testamentary trust in the state of Rhode Island and you move from the United States to Australia. It is more than likely that you would prefer to deal with a trust company in Australia than in Rhode Island. Not only does this avoid delays, but expense as well. This is one disadvantage of a testamentary trust. It locks you into a particular state or country.

The "living trust," on the other hand, can be moved anywhere in the world and is not administered by the probate or surrogate courts. It differs from the testamentary trust in that it is an entirely separate document and is not subject to probate proceedings. This has important consequences. To begin with, it means that the provisions contained in it are secret from the public, which can get a copy of a probate will from the court. This is not the case in a living trust, which is not filed in court.

Anyone who read in the newspapers about the Bing Crosby trust will remember that privacy was an important consideration with him. Secondly, a living trust provides a means of support for survivors while the will is going through probate proceedings, because funds may be placed in it during the lifetime of the grantor. For example, funds or life insurance may be placed in it which will provide for the emergency of untimely or eventual death. Life insurance that is placed in the trust can go immediately upon the death of the grantor to the surviving spouse. How often a widow has had to borrow funds while waiting for months for her husband's estate to be settled! The grief of her loss is then made even worse by financial worries. As mentioned before, the living trust can be moved anywhere in the world, provided that there is a clause in the trust stating that the trustee can be changed by the beneficiaries.

Another advantage of a living trust is that you can sell property to it and get paid off over a period of years. The result of this is frequently a significant tax saving, which can be of great benefit to a family. Also, as stated above, the trust can hold policies of insurance on the grantor's life, grantor's spouse, or grantor's children. Many people think there is no estate tax on insurance, but this is not the case. Insurance placed in a living trust is exempt from estate tax, whereas insurance not in a trust is taxed by the federal authorities, and in many states there is a state estate tax as well. Connecticut is one exception. Consult your attorney for your own state. Also, you can make gifts to the living trust under the gift tax exclusion and avoid tax. All of this should be done under the care of a skilled adviser. But even supposedly skilled advisers do not always cover all of these points. The purpose of this chapter is to make you aware of your options.

A living trust set up during your lifetime can be an important vehicle for anyone who may be thinking of making a bequest to you. This may be your husband, father, mother, grandmother, or anyone else. Such a bequest can go directly into your living trust and will only be taxed once, that is, before it goes into your trust. When you die it will not be taxed. However, if you can get up your courage to say to a relative who may be making a bequest to you, say your father, "Dad, if you plan to leave me anything in your will, you will do me a great favor if you leave instructions in your will that it go directly into a trust you set up in your will, or better yet, into a movable living trust set up by you now, and into which you can make a bequest to me if you so choose." In this latter case there will be a tax the first time round but not the second.

An estate tax is one levied by federal and state governments on bequests made in a will. In addition to estate taxes there is now a provision for taxing capital gains. The estate taxes plus the capital gains tax can eat up monumental amounts of an inheritance. In addition, an estate can be further eroded year by year by inflation. These are the difficult and unpleasant features of not leaving assets in trust for survivors. The subject of capital gains will be dealt with later in this chapter.

If stock is given to a trust more than three years prior to the death of the donor, it will not be subject to estate tax. Better yet, if the property is sold to the trust with payments made over a long period of years, the capital gains tax usually is sharply reduced and also long deferred. For example, if the seller is to be paid off over twenty years with 6-percent interest, the payment of the tax is deferred for an average period of ten years. Meanwhile the trust has the use of the money. In such case, if the trust resells the property, its capital gains tax is measured on the basis of the amount paid by the trust *or which the trust has promised to pay (even if the payment stretches over many years)*. This gives the beneficiaries the benefit of further inflationary increases in the value of the property "purchased" by it.

There is also a short-term trust, which a parent can set up for a period of years, usually at least ten years, or for remaining life. This keeps from your income assets being taxed to you and lets it accumulate for the education or for other benefits for your child or children, or other beneficiaries such as elderly parents. At the end of the ten-year period, in the case of children, or on the death of the elderly parent, the capital then reverts to you. In the meantime, the income goes to your child, children, or parent, and is taxed at their low bracket instead of in your higher bracket. This temporary trust is basically a vehicle to transfer income from one person to another without transferring ownership.

There is also the charitable trust. Many income and estate tax benefits result from turning property over to a charitable nonprofit institution by means of a charitable trust. It is possible to retain income from such a trust for your lifetime or that of a surviving spouse or other beneficiary.

An irrevocable living trust can use charitable remainder annuities, unitrusts, or pooled interest funds as an economy measure. These three types all have different specifications regarding the income you will be paid by the charity. A charitable remainder trust usually ranges, depending on your age, from a minimum of 5 percent to a maximum of between 7 to 9 percent. This is based on the value of the property at the time of transfer. A unitrust is the same thing, except that the value is recalculated every year. This can protect the donor-annuitant from inflation but also exposes her to the ravages of deflation. A pooled fund is one made up of the assets from several or many donors. They receive income based on the earnings of the pooled fund. These devices are of great value to people in their sixties, particularly for a single person (who cannot file a joint return), and especially if there are no dependants whom the donor wants to protect. In such case the donor may reserve an annuity measured not only by the life of the donor but also by the life of a dependant. This lessens the charitable deduction.

If a widow has three children, she can divide the property into three parts and, with regard to each of the parts, reserve an annuity for her lifetime with the remainder continuing in each separate case for each of the children. This reduces the amount of the charitable deduction. Bequests of a charitable remainder annuity can also save estate taxes. For example, a husband may make a bequest to such a trust reserving for his widow an annual income equal to 5 percent of the value of the assets, and immunize such a trust to a substantial degree from estate taxes. The amount of protection depends on the age of the beneficiary at the time of death. The older the beneficiary the greater the amount of deduction, since the charity will succeed to the entire property that much earlier. Most charities, including particularly universities, have more extensive descriptions of how these work, but you must also consult your tax adviser, since this is one of the most complicated sections of the tax law.

Any trust may be revocable or irrevocable. In the revocable trust the grantor has the power to amend or revoke it during her lifetime. In an irrevocable trust the grantor may not revoke or amend it. The difference between these two forms is very great, particularly from a tax point of view. For example, you can give property to an irrevocable trust and avoid paying either gift or estate tax on it.

If you want to save possibly huge expenses and

delays in the probate administration of your estate, you can have a revocable trust which becomes irrevocable at death. Such a trust does not save the grantor any income or estate taxes but permits the family to get acquainted with the trustee during her lifetime during which time you can yourself change the trustee. The chief advantage is that it simplifies administration problems and reduces expenses at death.

ESTATE ASSETS

When you decide that you want your assets held in a trust for future distribution, the first thing to do is make a list of what will go in it. What goes into a trust is called the "principal." Principal is the capital of an estate or trust. It may be cash, stocks, bonds, real estate, royalties, or life insurance. All these things are called "capital assets." When an estate is being settled and the will directs that assets be "poured over" into a trust, it often happens that assets must be sold. Capital gain is the gain realized from the sale of a capital asset for more than its "basis."

In estate situations the capital gains tax gets very complicated. If you inherited something prior to January 1, 1977, the basis would be the value at which the property was taxed in the estate of the person from whom you inherited it. If the person died after December 31, 1976, the basis would be what it was selling at on December 31, 1976 if it was stock listed on a national exchange. Otherwise the basis would be the value at December 31, 1976, computed in a very complicated fashion, depending on how long it had been held altogether, both before and after December 31, 1976. For anyone but a certified public accountant, the only important thing to do is get your hands on the records and let someone who knows how do the rest. This is one reason you must keep records of acquisition dates and costs. These rules are presently being reviewed by Congress.

If a trustee is given discretion to take capital and distribute it to a beneficiary in addition to the annual income from the trust, this is called "invasion of principal." This discretionary power is to permit the trustee to take care of emergency situations or because the income is insufficient. Sometimes the beneficiary has the right to invade the principal. In the latter instance, great care should be taken so that the beneficiary is not taxed on property she was entitled to take if she needed it, but in fact did not take.

On the subject of trusts there are a number of modifications and definitions that are useful to know about. The word "accumulation" refers to the case when a trust does not distribute all of its income currently. The portion of income which is left undistributed is called an "accumulation."

The word "necessities" often turns up. These are sums which one person is required by law to provide for another person. In most states, and subject to the passage of the Equal Rights Amendment, a husband is required to support a wife if she has no earning power, or, in some states, no assets of her own. It is also required by law in most states that a child up to eighteen shall be supported. Support includes food, housing, clothing, medical care, and depending on state law, education. The states are divided as to whether or not a college education is a "necessity." However, in most states, a child is not entitled to support after reaching age eighteen, and, therefore, in most instances a college education is not a "necessity." Nevertheless, most parents treat it as a matter of prime concern to provide for education, including college education, for their children. This is important because if a grantor sets up a trust making the parent a trustee and the trust pays for "necessities" for which the parent is personally responsible, the parent may be taxed on that portion of the income of the trust that was used to pay for necessities. This is true if the husband or father, as the trustee, used trust property to pay for necessities which he otherwise was obliged to provide.

"Community property" (as discussed in detail in a separate chapter) is another important concept in the subject of wills and trusts. This is a provision of law which divides property earned during marriage equally between husband and wife. Community property is the law only in some states, which are: Arizona, California, Idaho, Louisiana, Nevada, New Mexico, Texas, and Washington. The result of this is that if a person dies in a community property state, one half of the estate attributable to earnings during the marriage becomes the outright property of the surviving spouse. "Surviving spouse" means a husband or wife who survives, that is, a surviving widow or widower.

"Marital deduction" is important to know about. In 1948, Congress provided that a person did not have to pay estate tax to the extent that up to one half of his estate was bequeathed to a surviving spouse. In 1976, this amount was increased to $250,000 or one half of the estate, whichever is the greater. This bequest can be outright or in trust. If in trust, the surviving spouse must receive the income regularly and must have the right to designate who will be the beneficiary at the time such surviving spouse dies. By this means the tax on this partner can be deferred until the death of the surviving spouse and the total tax reduced, since each half is taxed in lower percentages. But to leave the entire estate outright to the surviving spouse is terribly expensive. Then one half the estate is taxed at the first death and the entire estate is taxed at the second death, if not spent or given away. Thus it is possible to pay 50 percent more than you should. The best procedure is to leave one half to the surviving spouse in a marital trust (described above) and one half to the surviving spouse and your descendants in a family trust. Unless the estate of yourself and your husband (including life insurance) is under $200,000, beware of a lawyer who prepares a simple will leaving everything outright without trusts.

A "general power of appointment" is one of the powers that may be included in a trust which allows the person named to do with the property (stock, real estate, cash, or any other bequest) whatever she pleases, either during her lifetime, or by her will in her estate after her death. Anyone in the world can be the beneficiary of such a power. The person who has this power must pay taxes on the property over which she has the general power of appointment, whether or not she exercises it. A power given to a beneficiary to withdraw from the capital of a trust for her benefit in her own discretion is the same as a general power of appointment, since the beneficiary can withdraw the money and give it to anyone she chooses.

A "limited power of appointment" is the same as a general power, except that a person to whom the power is given is restricted to a defined class of people, such as her descendants, or any other group as long as this group does not include the person who has the limited power, her creditors, or her estate. The exercise of a limited power of appointment has no adverse tax consequences.

The word "gift" in connection with wills and trusts is the voluntary transfer of property during life if not in exchange for a payment equal to its market value. "Market value" is what property could be sold for to a stranger.

For those who are in a position to make tax-free gifts to their children, there is what is called the "gift tax exclusion." This is currently $3,000 a year for each person giving property and for each person receiving property. Accordingly, if a husband and wife have a son and a daughter, the annual excludable amount is $12,000, as follows:

Gift of husband to daughter	$3,000
Gift of husband to son	3,000

Gift of wife to daughter	3,000
Gift of wife to son	3,000
Annual total	$12,000

The wife's gift does not have to be made out of her own assets. She can "lend" her exclusion to her husband and vice-versa. The exclusion increases as the number of donors increase or the number of donees is increased. For example, if there is a generous aunt, she can give $3,000 to the son and another $3,000 to the daughter. If there is a generous uncle, he can do likewise. Also, if there is a grandchild, he or she can be given $3,000 from each donor every year. If the gift is to a trust, the rules are very technical as to whether such a gift is eligible for an "exclusion." The whole series of gifts can be repeated every year. "Donor" is the person who makes the gift. "Donee" is the person who receives the gift. A "gift tax" is a tax levied (subject to a credit which defers the tax until it reaches a given amount varying annually. By 1981 the credit will cover gifts or bequests up to $175,000.) by the federal government and in some cases by the state government on gifts over the exclusion.

There is also a lifetime $100,000 credit on gifts from one spouse to another.

Finally there is the interesting subject of the "discretionary spray trust." This is one in which the trustee is given discretion as to whether or not income will be accumulated or distributed and when this will be done. It also frequently permits the trustee to decide whether circumstances require that one beneficiary receive more or less than another beneficiary, usually on the basis of the needs of the beneficiaries and their financial responsibility. Such trusts usually provide for an invasion of principal where deemed necessary by the trustee. It is very important that such powers be vested in an "independent trustee," as defined earlier in this chapter. Otherwise, all kinds of tax traps can open up for the grantor and beneficiary of the trust.

If you are married, it is of the utmost importance that *you and your husband* confer jointly with an attorney specializing in estate planning and develop a program which will provide for you and your children fairly, adequately, and without enormous tax-wastage. This should be tied in with your family life insurance program (with the aid of an insurance expert) and your employee benefits. Start thinking about it in your twenties or thirties, or as soon as you can. Your husband needs your signature every year on his joint tax return (see chapter 11, "Sharing It"). You are his partner and he cannot expect you to take the risk of a joint return without letting you see his will and estate and insurance plan, and having it fully explained to you.

This chapter can only be considered as a bird's-eye view of the subject of inheritance, but it does outline many options that are open to you. It stresses the importance of making a will, of keeping careful records of assets, of the tax opportunities inherent in trusts, and above all, of planning ahead with thoughtfulness and care.

Most people who set up trusts put them in their wills as *testamentary trusts*. As previously explained, however, there can be enormous family security advantages, tax advantages, and administrative economies achieved through the use of *living trusts*, that is, trusts set up outside of a will during the lifetime of the person who creates the trust, namely, the grantor or settlor.

We shall end this chapter with a summary of twenty-nine uses of *living trusts*. Twenty-four of the trusts listed will be irrevocable. During the lifetime of the grantor there need not be a lot of money or other property in the irrevocable trusts, but anything that is given or sold to such trusts cannot be taken back, and must be used for trust purposes. On the other hand, in the instances in which it is advantageous to use *revocable trusts*, the grantor can cancel or amend them during her lifetime, but faces tax disadvantages.

What Irrevocable Living Trusts Can Do

1. *Provide an annuity for a single woman.*
2. *Fund education for children or grandchildren.* An educational fund for grandchildren can be much more serviceable than a direct bequest to the parent of the children.
3. *Free pension and profit-sharing plans from estate tax.* A trust, if made the beneficiary of the executive's pension or profit-sharing trust death benefits, can avoid estate tax not only on the death of the executive but on the death of the surviving spouse.
4. *Free insurance from estate tax.* Insurance is taxable to the estate of the insured if she retains any incident of ownership. If the insurance is given to the spouse, the spouse's estate will pay a heavy tax on it and it will be subject to the claims of a subsequent spouse. The use of the irrevocable living trust avoids tax in the estate of the husband or the wife. This applies to ordinary life, group, and accidental death insurance.
5. *Make tax-free gifts.* This procedure can remove from the taxable estate, without gift tax, the sum of $5,000 per year, multiplied by the number of children or grandchildren, and multiplied by the number of nieces and nephews. A father, with a wife, two children, two nieces and four grandchildren, can free from estate and gift tax up to $45,000 *annually.* In the case of an unmarried donor, this gift is limited to $3,000 per donee annually. This procedure, in the example given, would save at least $12,000 annually in the estate taxes besides having all the other advantages of irrevocable living trusts. (The gift by two donors could be $6,000, but if the gift ex-

ceeds the greater of $5,000 or 5 percent of
the trust principal, it creates gift tax problems for the trust beneficiary under Section
2514(e) of the Internal Revenue Code.)

6. *Make the trust movable.* If a trust is set up
   during life and separate from a will, it can be
   moved from one state to another. This mobility is denied in most states to testamentary
   trusts.

7. *Provide privacy.* Anyone can see the contents
   of a will, along with the contents of a trust
   set up in a will, when filed for probate. But
   the public cannot see the contents of *living
   trusts*. The late Bing Crosby got privacy in
   this way. His will provided that his estate be
   "poured over" into a separate trust, and this
   the public could not see.

8. Provide the means to make prudent investments for heirs.

9. Prevent a subsequent spouse from disinherit-
   ing your children to the extent of one third
   of your estate.

10. *"Sprinkle" estate assets* (income and princi-
    pal) among various members of the family.
    It is hard to tell in advance what will be the
    future needs of a spouse and children. The
    irrevocable living trust can distribute accord-
    ing to the financial and emotional situation of
    beneficiaries.

11. *Time the distribution of estate assets.* It is
    impossible to foresee the best age for distribu-
    tion of capital to children. Rather than have
    funds distributed at a predetermined age, an
    irrevocable living trust permits the distribu-
    tion to be matched to the financial maturity
    and needs of the children as they develop.

12. *Hold insurance to pay estate tax.* Frequently,
    a widow's estate tax can be higher than that
    of her deceased husband. This is due to the

fact that she would have inherited one half of her husband's estate and may have had other assets of her own, such as savings accounts, earnings, and other inheritances. For this reason, the irrevocable living trust should own insurance on the life of the widow in order to pay her estate tax. Her husband had the advantage of the marital deduction, which she would not have unless she were to remarry and predecease her second husband.

13. *Hold bequests*. Trusts created during life provide an excellent repository for bequests from parents or in-laws.

14. *Shelter family partnership assets*. The trust, as a member of a family partnership, can shelter assets from capital gains, estate and gift taxes, and also sharply reduce income taxes.

15. *Provide an already established vehicle* for a widow to pour over funds at her decease. A trust set up by her husband is familiar to her, and she would not have to go to the expense of creating a new trust.

16. *Defer generation-skipping tax*. A trust, if properly programmed, can defer the impact of the generation-skipping tax, newly provided for by tax legislation, until the death of the last surviving child of the trust creator.

17. *Shelter capital gains*. An irrevocable living trust can be used as a means to shelter capital gains taxes, which could ordinarily carry a tax running from 25 to 40 percent. It can also reduce tax on the disposition of an ordinary income item such as inventory, copyrights, or property on which accelerated depreciation has been taken, or production equipment.

18. *Reduce capital gains*. An irrevocable living trust can also sharply reduce capital gains

taxes by purchasing property in exchange for its long-term installment notes.

19. *Avoid tax on sale of assets by decedent's heirs.* Since December 31, 1976, there has been a tax on appreciated assets which are sold by decedent's heirs. These can be reduced or avoided by sale via a trust.

20. *Provide a superior way to make gifts or bequests to individuals or trusts.* Family members can make interest-free loans (under the *Crown* case) to trusts or lend them collateral. The trusts could then invest and accumulate the proceeds or use them to insure the lives of the lendors or any other member of the family.

21. *Provide funds for an elderly parent or other dependent.* An irrevocable living trust can be set up for at least ten years, or the balance of the life of the relative, even though the life expectancy of the beneficiary may be less than ten years. The income is paid to the beneficiary and taxed at his or her lower brackets. The principal reverts to the donor when the trust terminates on the death of the relative or at the end of ten years. This is a more advantageous way to provide for a dependent, rather than have the donor pay a heavy tax on her income and then pay over money for supporting the relative. This form of trust has no estate tax saving value, except that the income which is paid over to the beneficiary does not become part of the estate of the donor. It also removes the onus of writing checks for one's relative, who is constantly reminded of his or her dependency. Getting a check from a trust company gives a greater feeling of dignity.

22. *Provide short-term funds for any family member.* The ten-year (or more) irrevocable liv-

ing trust may be set up for a member of the family in lower tax brackets who will receive only the income from the trust. When the trust is terminated the principal will revert to the donor. The funds may also be paid to the guardian of a minor child. As mentioned in the preceding item, this trust has no estate tax saving value, except that the income which is paid to the beneficiary does not become part of the estate of the donor.

23. *Benefit dependents by purchase and lease back.* A professional or business person such as a physician who owns a professional building (or an individual entrepreneur) can sell the building to a trust for the benefit of his dependents and then lease it back. The trust gets the rent but bases its depreciation on the new cost which it is paying out as a capital gain to the vendor. This not only can eliminate from the estate of the vendor subsequent increases in the value of the building, but also gives the vendor capital gains instead of ordinary taxable income. This can be done with children but should not be done with a spouse as a beneficiary. The rent, largely sheltered from tax by the higher depreciation, can also help support the beneficiary. This issue has been bitterly contested by the Internal Revenue Service, and there are court decisions on both sides of the matter. The transaction will stand up only if it is programmed most carefully and correctly by tax counsel, but the advantages are so great that the procedure warrants exploration in depth.

What Revocable Living Trusts Can Do

1. Permit a family to evaluate the performance

of a trust company during the lifetime of the main provider.

2. Provide major estate administration economies on the death of the creator of the trust by keeping major assets out of the probate procedure and continuing the administration of the assets under the trust.

3. *Avoid "ancillary" probate costs.* If a deceased person has substantial assets in some other state (such as a valuable summer residence), his death would require probate of his estate in the state where he resided plus "ancillary" administration in the other state where his real property or some other assets might be located. Placing such assets in a revocable trust retains control over them during the lifetime of the owner and involves no gift tax. But it does save the expense of ancillary probate administration.

4. *Avoid "double domicile."* A grave danger, particularly in the sun belt, is double domicile, with two states claiming that a decedent was an exclusive resident of each. (The U.S. Supreme Court has intervened in the case of Howard Hughes to decide whether Texas or California can claim an inheritance tax.) If a person moves from one state to another for professional or private reasons, leaving property behind him, this might require ancillary probate and invite a claim by the former state that domicile in that state had not been terminated; and that a second state inheritance tax was due to it. Usually the old state gets involved when assets in that state are transferred. If such assets are already in a revocable trust, the likelihood of this kind of trouble is greatly reduced.

10

Retiring on It

At some time every employee (whether it be the woman, her husband, or father or mother) will leave the job. Termination may be by death (see chapter on life insurance), involuntary termination, resignation, or retirement.

This chapter is about retirement—your own or that of a member of your family.

With the vast increase of the over-fifty-five age group, support for the retiree is all the more important. It may be you. It may be your husband or it may be your father or mother. The retirement income of parents can be important to you because if they are not provided for, you may have to pitch in.

For medium and lower income brackets, social security is the rock on which financial security of the retiree is *initially* built.

The various factors influencing the amount of your social security benefits are enormously complicated. It will vary with legislation, with income, with age of retirement, the earned income after retirement, and with the status of the payee, be she employee, or the wife, widow, or other dependent of some other covered employee. These factors are so numerous that it would be impossible to enumerate them here, particularly since the rules are frequently altered by Congress. We suggest that the retiree and her family from time to time go to the nearest social security office and find out the various alternatives of social security as to commencement date, duration, amount, and so on. On the question of amount, it may be stated that with inflation, the amount of benefits and the amount of taxes levied against (1) the employee and (2) her employer have been constantly increasing. The only thing to do is to discover what the benefits would be under the present social security legislation and to hope that they will, at least in part, keep up with inflation.

Large numbers of people are covered by governmental retirement programs other than social security. These are mostly civil service employees. If you are one of these, it is advisable that you speak to the appropriate person in your organization and ascertain the same information. (See chapter 2.)

Apart from social security or other governmental retirement benefits, we have the vast area of private pensions. Retirement benefits may be financed by the employer, by the employee, or by both.

If you are self-employed, it is possible to set aside annually up to 15 percent of your compensation, but not more than $7,500. This sum is deductible from your taxable income. And accumulated income from its investment is free of tax until distribution upon retirement or death. Calculations of how much can be accumulated, depending on amount contributed, number of years of contribution, and income earned by the contribution can be made by computer for you easily and at no cost through any one of the competing agencies that would like to have you deposit your money with them. These include banks, savings institutions, life insurance companies, and mutual funds.

However, if your income is over $25,000 or $30,000 a year (before taxes), you can accomplish more by incorporating yourself and then having your own corporation install a standard, qualified pension plan of the kind we shall discuss. The reasons for this are that a corporate-funded pension plan permits the deposit of larger amounts (if you can afford it) and thus larger tax savings and larger tax-free accumulation of capital. Authors, entertainers, physicians, dentists, and other professionals, public secretaries (individually or in groups) and almost anybody (except a housewife—and this should be remedied) may be incorporated. The corporation can then pay a salary to its employee and, as we shall discuss, supplement it by a tax-free deposit (which is also tax deductible by the corporation) into a qualified pension plan. Many other insurance, sick plan, and other benefits can be achieved by incorporation. Every year thousands of individuals are incorporated and go to work for their own corporation, and with a knowledgeable attorney and accountant, this is a fairly simple task. Such pension plans are not only more lucrative, they permit a greater flexibility in investment, time, and retirement benefits. Any woman who is self-employed and whose taxable income, together with that of her husband, exceeds $40,000 or $50,000 will find that she is unnecessarily missing thousands of dollars of tax benefits if she remains unincorporated. At the very least this should be made the subject of efficient professional counseling.

For the individual who is employed by somebody else and where there is no pension plan, it is possible to deposit, depending on income, up to $1,500 annually on a tax-deductible basis with tax-free accumulations. But if a woman is employed by an organization that does not have a qualified plan, she should look for another job, unless her period of employment will be very short, or if her cash compensation is considerably higher than standard for the job or unless she loves her job and is getting other advantages from it.

We come now to the standard qualified retirement plan.

These, sometimes financed solely by the employer and occasionally financed by contributions from the employer plus contributions by the employee, are always an extraordinarily important element in any financial plan.

There are tens of thousands of plans, and almost all of them differ in some respect or another. In 1974, Congress enacted legislation which massively altered the law as to such pension plans. Details as to qualification, benefits, forfeitures on termination of employment before retirement, investment, trustee conduct, and the like were provided in a law of encyclopedic proportions. The purpose of the law was primarily to protect the average employee from the loss of her retirement security through discrimination, forfeiture, bad investments, or otherwise. Unfortunately, by the time the legislation had worked its way through Congress, with each Congressman making his own contribution, the reporting requirements became so complicated that many moderate or smaller companies found that compliance was just too expensive and dropped their plans. This is unfortunate and unnecessary. With careful search, even a small corporation can discover professional specialists in these fields who are sufficiently computerized to make compliance relatively easy and economical. Moreover, there is a good chance that Congress will become a little bit more sensible and not throw out the baby with the bathwater, thereby avoiding eliminating more pension benefits than Congress is saving.

There are two basic types of qualified retirement plans. These are

1. The Defined Benefit Plan

2.   The Defined Contribution Plan

DEFINED BENEFIT PLAN

Here the planners (usually management, and sometimes unions, guided by actuaries, attorneys, accountants, trust officers, insurance experts, and investment counselors) agree on a formula for benefits. These are usually determined by a percentage of compensation, years of service, and retirement age. Here are some typical formulas: a fixed percentage of average salary, such as 40 or 50 percent; a similar percentage by using the five highest years of compensation; a percentage of compensation such as 1 or 2 percent for each year of service with the employer.

A critical variation of the price formula is the plan which "integrates" social security with the employer-provided benefits. The basic concept here is to continue privately supplied retirement benefits where social security leaves off. For example, if the plan provides for a defined benefit of $1,000 a month and the "credited" social security benefit (usually not the exact amount of social security) is $250 a month, then the employer will have to plan to accumulate only enough money in the plan to provide $750 a month, which together with $250 of credited social security is the designated amount of defined benefit.

The percentages allowed by the Internal Revenue Service as a condition of approving a plan as qualified, vary as social security benefits vary and as the thinking of the IRS pundits changes from year to year. Usually once a format has been approved by the IRS, changes in the social security integration requirements will not be enforced against the already-qualified plan in the absence of very extensive modifications of the plan by the employer itself.

With respect to all of the legal requirements as to a plan, great care should be exercised before substantially modifying a plan. The employer or the employee may be losing the benefit of an already-qualified plan which would not again be able to obtain approval. For example, in the 1974 legislation, the Congress put a ceiling of $75,000 on pension benefits attributable to the employer's contribution, but provided that if, in September 1973 (when the proposal was first brought up in Congress) there was a larger pension under a qualified plan, such a pension could be continued, unless the plan was substantially amended. For those of you who grieve for executives whose retirement pension was limited to a paltry $75,000 a year, let us give one crumb of comfort. There was, of course, a cost-of-living adjustment. In just a few years this increased the maximum allowable amount by approximately $15,000 and, with continuing inflation, will probably increase even more.

Of course, the defined benefit can also be predicated upon the contributions of employees. The portion of compensation contributed into a retirement plan by an employee is not tax deductible by the employee. The contribution by the employer is tax deductible by the employer. This makes many "contributory" plans unattractive, although some managements emphatically claim that benefits not paid for in part by the beneficiary are not adequately appreciated.

Once the defined benefit has been determined, an actuary can work out how much has to be contributed annually in order to accumulate, at a stipulated rate of return on the investment, a large enough sum to pay the pension for the life expectancy of the retiree. A retiree is allowed to stipulate that his benefits are to continue for the period of survival of his spouse or other beneficiary. Of course, this reduces the amount of the retirement income. As a rough rule of thumb, if this survivorship option is selected, the husband must agree to take 20 percent less if the wife is the same age as he (because of the longer life expectancy of women) and must subtract another 2 percent for every year by which she is his junior. Thus, a man who has a wife five years younger than he must reduce his pension of, say, $1,000 a month to $700 a month if he wants to have it continue for his wife's survival. The aforementioned 20 percent accounts for $200 of this reduction and 2 percentage points for each year of the five years by which she is his junior accounts for another 10 percent, or 30 percent in all, thus, bringing the pension down to $700 a month. It is often better planning for the husband to take an unreduced pension and to provide survivorship benefits either through insurance on his life, which he purchases, or by a survivorship program independent of the pension plan, which the employer may (but is not required) to provide.

Although employers are required to furnish all participating employees with detailed booklets as to their benefits, it has been our experience that very few, if any, employees are remotely aware of what their pension benefits will be. This applies even to important financial executives of huge corporations. The wives of such employees are even worse informed. Any person of caution would be disturbed if an individual knew as little about the amount she and her husband had in the bank as such persons know about the amount of their pension benefits. Yet the pension benefits will be vastly more important in any financial program at retirement than the amount that may be on deposit in a bank.

Both husband and wife should sit down with the appropriate executive in the employer company and find out the answers to the questions raised by the foregoing comments. While doing this it should be ascertained what adjustment will be made to retirement benefits in case of early retirement, say, at sixty-two or sixty or even fifty-five.

Another important thing to find out is what death benefits are incorporated into the plan in case the employee dies before retirement. Many plans provide no death benefit and many surviving spouses discover too late that they are facing penury because of premature death of the employee without adequate death protection either under the pension plan or supplied by group life insurance or by privately owned insurance. This area of information is one of the top priorities in your financial self-education (see chapter on life insurance).

The funds contributed by the employer (and sometimes the employee) to build up the reserve necessary to finance the retirement benefit can be handled in many ways. One fashion is not to have any trustee at all and simply to buy an annuity contract from an insurance company. This has the advantage of an assurance that the pension will be paid at a predetermined cost no matter how long the employee (or surviving spouse) may live. With many companies the specter of being forced to contribute large, additional sums because employees are living longer than expected is a serious one, and there is a preference for placing this risk in the hands of an insurance company. With noninsured pension plans the cost to American industry for the discovery of a cure for cancer, heart disease, or high blood pressure could be bankruptcy. Apart from inflation, unemployment and labor relations, this is the most serious financial threat facing the American economy, yet it is the least appreciated.

The trust companies, on the other hand, argue that their earnings can be higher than those of an insurance company and that the pension costs will thus be less. The trust companies, however, do not guarantee that they will have enough money in the fund to pay the pension for life. Nevertheless this is a fact of great importance. After many years of work in this field we have come to the conclusion that it depends on the individual trust company and the individual insurance company. Some trust companies do excellently, others do terribly. Some insurance earnings are significantly and decisively higher than those of other Medicare insurance companies. The form of investment is a matter of constant appraisal and reappraisal.

If an annuity contract is not purchased from an insurance company, there must be a trustee. The trustee may be a trust company or one or more individuals or some combination of both types. Here again it is a matter of individual appraisal of performance. This area of pension planning has been severely regulated by the 1974 Act. It is most important that the investment record of a given trust company or insurance company be checked out. There are several national publications that do just this on an annual or more frequent basis.

One form of investment for a pension plan balances off the various factors in planning. One type of program has part of the money, such as one half going into insurance premiums, and the remainder going into a trust fund. A specialized type of insurance policy provides that if the employee dies before retirement the insurance company will pay substantial tax-free insurance benefits to the employee's family. The balance in the trust fund then is used to help finance the pension costs of the surviving employees. At retirement, if the employee has survived, there is an option to use the cash value in the insurance policy (see explanation of cash value in the chapter on life insurance) together with the funds held by the trustee—including the accumulated income thereon—to convert the life insurance contract into an annuity contract whereby the insurance company will pay to the employee and any contingent survivor beneficiary the stipulated pension.

The great advantage of this "split funded" program is that it provides insurance protection against premature death and for unexpected extended survivorship, while permitting half the contribution to be used by the trust company in the hope of a larger "side fund" earned with the contributions and thus reducing the total costs.

In our opinion this combination program protects against many contingencies otherwise not touched. Its disadvantages lie in the cost of administration, with giant companies having thousands of hundreds of thousands of employees. It is important that trust companies and insurance companies collaborate so that the benefits of split funding can be made available to the very large company as well as to the small.

DEFINED CONTRIBUTION PLANS

In such plans the contribution is determined first, and the amount of benefits then predicated on the amount of the fixed contributions plus earnings thereon. This is contrasted with the Defined Benefit Plan, where you first determine the ultimate pension and *then* determine the contributions necessary to provide the targeted benefits.

We have discussed the target or defined benefit plans. We shall now discuss the defined contribution plans. These fall mainly into four categories.

1. "Money purchase" plans
2. "Profit sharing" plans
3. Stock bonus plans
4. Employee stock ownership plans (ESOP)

The first thing to consider is that defined benefit, or target, plans are more favorable for people over thirty-five, and defined contribution plans more favorable for people thirty-five or less.

For example, if a stockholder is twenty-five years of age and earns $36,000 a year and is targeted for a pension of $2,000 a month at age sixty-five, he needs to have the corporation contribute $3,240 a year, even if only a 4-percent increment is to be earned, and a lesser amount if 5-percent or more can be earned. In any event he needs a capital of $320,000 at age sixty-five to provide the pension. But he has forty years of contributions *plus nontaxable earnings on those contributions* in which to accumulate it.

The following schedule (for a man earning $36,000) shows what happens at different ages, first with a pension plan (on the same assumptions as stated) and then with a profit-sharing plan where the maximum tax-deductible deposit may be no more than 15 percent of annual income, which in this case would be $5,400 a year. The comparative table of annual contributions is as follows:

Age	Pension Plan	Profit-Sharing Plan
25	$3,040	$5,400
35	5,140	5,400
45	9,690	5,400
55	24,030	5,400

(In the case of a woman, the amounts are decreased to approximately those of a man three years younger than the woman)

It is thus apparent that more money may be contributed under a pension plan than under a profit-sharing plan if the employee is over thirty-five when entering the plan.

You may have nothing to say about this if you are an average employee in a large corporation, but it is very important to you if you or your family controls the corporation, particularly a small corporation with one or two or three employees. If you have no say in the matter, consider a change to a more generous employer.

Money Purchase Plan

Here a stipulated amount, up to 10 percent of compensation, is contributed annually. This type of plan is not as favorable for the employee as the target plan. Its only virtue is its simplicity and the fact that a given amount is contributed every year. While it can be a useful supplement to other retirement plans, standing alone it's the least useful type of plan, at least from the employee point of view.

Profit-Sharing Plans

Here the employer is permitted to contribute and deduct part of its net earnings before taxes, up to a maximum deductible sum of 15 percent of the compensation of participants in any one year. (The 15 percent is a percentage of salary, not profit.) The contribution may be determined annually by the board of directors, or it can be on a formula basis such as "5 percent of corporate earnings before taxes, but not more than 15 percent of compensation." There are many other formulas which can be used, such as formulas that reflect increased productivity. The disadvantage of a formula plan is that it is more rigid than the year-by-year plan. While the formula plan may be changed, it is usually bad psychology to reduce the formula. The advantage of the increased productivity formula is that it gives the employees something concrete to shoot for.

With the 15 percent of compensation ceiling, if earnings are low in one year and less than 15 percent of compensation is contributed, then the corporation can contribute over 15 percent (but not in excess of 30 percent in any one year). For example, if only 5 percent of compensation is contributed in one year, then 15 percent plus 10 percent—or 25 percent—may be contributed in any subsequent year.

The major advantage of a profit-sharing plan as against a fixed-benefit pension plan is that contribution can be adjusted for poor business. However, this can be a fallacy, particularly in a small corporation. A well-designed pension plan bases benefits on compensation and bases contributions on benefits. Thus, with a one- or two-person corporation, if business slacks off, the owners/employees can reduce their compensation during the poor years and thus in turn reduce the contribution. Therefore, if you are an owner/employee over thirty-five years of age, do not accept the statement that a profit-sharing plan is more flexible than a pension plan. Show the foregoing statement to your adviser and ask the adviser to illustrate how this would work at various assumed rates of corporate earnings, compensation, and ages. It is ill advised to give up the larger deductible contributions available under a pension plan in order to go for the apparent greater flexibility of the profit-sharing plan without a thorough review of the foregoing points.

Stock Bonus Plan

This, of course, is just like a profit-sharing plan, except that the corporation contributes into the trust its own stock rather than cash. It gets a tax deduction for the value of the stock but doesn't have to lay out cash. Its net cash position is therefore *increased* rather than *decreased*, as is the case with all other types of qualified plans. Furthermore, when the stock is distributed at retirement or termination of employment, the employee's tax is based on the value of the stock when it was contributed and he does not pay a tax on the excess until he actually sells the stock.

Furthermore, this type of plan has a double incentive. The employee is inspired to contribute to earnings of the corporation by hard work so that the amount deposited in the stock bonus plan will be increased. Since the stock of the corporation is contributed he has a second incentive to build up the value of this stock for future advantages. Sears has made millionaires out of a large number of its employees, who were not necessarily all top executives, through this kind of a plan, and it is believed that this double incentive did much to put Sears where it is today.

ESOP

The initials above stand for the name "Employee Stock Ownership Plan." This, of course, is much like a stock bonus plan, except that the corporation may, if it chooses, contribute cash into the plan and then the cash can be used to buy the stock of the corporation either on the open market (if it is a publicly held corporation) or from individual stockholders. The money may also be used to pay premiums on life insurance carried on the stockholders. The proceeds of this insurance can be used to buy stock from the estate of a deceased stockholder and put such stock into the employee trust. This has great tax benefits.

This type of plan has many advantages. It has the advantage of a stock bonus plan but has additional advantages in providing a market for the stock for its existing stockholders while giving the corporation the right to buy this stock, through the plan, on a tax-deductible basis. Ordinarily, if a corporation desires to buy the stock of a deceased shareholder so that his estate may pay inheritance taxes, it may not deduct the purchase price of that stock. Also, such a transaction is subject to many tax complexities. If there is an ESOP and the corporation can make the purchase through an ESOP trust *on a tax-deductible basis* at a corporate tax rate of 50 percent, the stock thus costs the corporation one half as much, after taxes, as stock purchased in the ordinary way.

Moreover, this type of plan is looked on very favorably by the government. The 1974 Act, which put all kinds of complications and hurdles in the way of the ordinary pension or profit-sharing plan, in several key places exempted ESOP from its restrictions and requirements. Also, Congress has actually increased the "investment tax credit" (given to taxpayers when they acquire equipment such as new machine tools) in cases where the corporation has an ESOP.

Such programs were described by one of the authors in an article of the *Harvard Business Review* in March 1953, but only in recent years has the idea caught on. It has been particularly popularized on the West Coast.

It is recommended that if you are the owner of a

corporation that you seriously examine this opportunity. If you are an employee of a corporation, it will do you no harm to give a copy of this book to your boss with these pages particularly noted.

TAX QUALIFICATION

The government is very uptight to make sure that all these types of plans not be used to discriminate against lower-paid employees and that the plans be carefully and faithfully maintained to protect the employee. It would take several books the size of this volume to explain all the requirements in various laws enacted by Congress in this connection. We will mention only a few highlights.

1. The plan must include all full-time employees (1,000 hours a year) if they are twenty-five or over and less than sixty-five.
2. No greater benefits can be given to high-paid employees than to low-paid employees other than proportioning the pension or contribution to the amount of compensation received. Also, the plan may be "integrated" with social security. (This does provide for further increase of proportionate contribution for higher-paid employees.)
3. The rights of a participant may not be arbitrarily terminated just because the employee terminates her employment, voluntarily or involuntarily. There are three different formulas for such "vesting." Vesting means a point at which pension benefits earned cease to be forfeitable for any reason. The vesting formula depends on the number of years of service with the corporation or participation in the plan, so that the employee is more and more vested as each year passes. At the least favor-

able formula (from the employee point of view) the rights of an employee must be fully vested by the time she has been a participant in the plan for fifteen years.

4. The plan must be carefully maintained and faithfully administered. Any kind of self-dealing is prohibited. Regular reports must be made to the IRS and the Department of Labor, and most pension plans are "insured" by a government-supervised insurance company.

If two or more corporations or other business entities are controlled by the same people, they must *all* conform to these rules as if they were a single employer. For example, if three men own all the stock of two corporations but receive high salaries from only one corporation, they may not install a juicy plan in the corporation where they are receiving high compensation and a niggardly plan in the other. The question of "common control" is subject to very complex rules and has continually been litigated, but watch out for this.

TAXATION OF DISTRIBUTIONS

Cash distributions of benefits are subject to income tax only when the distribution is made. It used to be advantageous to take the full amount standing to your credit in a lump sum, but this is no longer the case, unless the amount thus taken is turned over into a special form of accumulation ("roll over") annuity which defers the taxation and accumulates more income on the fund until cash distribution is made at a later date.

Usually the best way to take distribution is over a period of years. This can be either for the life of the employee, and some contingent beneficiary such as a surviving spouse or child, or for life, with a minimum fixed period of years, such as ten years.

DEATH TAXES

A tremendous advantage of these qualified plans is that if the distribution is taken over more than one year and the participant dies before complete distribution, any amount not yet paid out to the beneficiary is exempt from an estate tax. If part of the plan is in the form of insurance on the life of the participant, the proceeds of the insurance are also free from estate tax (unless paid to the executors or administrators of the employee) and are also free of income tax, except for a tax on the cash value of the insured's policy. This is one of the most effective tax shelters that have been allowed to continue in our law.

With wealthy people it is usually better to have the benefits paid not to family members directly but to trusts for their benefit. This is particularly so if the spouse is the principal beneficiary. With such a program the proceeds are not only exempt from tax at the death of the employee but do not even pick up a tax when the spouse dies. This becomes significant when the aggregate assets of a family exceed about $200,000 including insurance and death benefits from pension plans.

NON-QUALIFIED PLANS

We will take just a paragraph to discuss these. Sometimes employers want to benefit specially selected employees rather than the entire rank and file. Such a plan may not qualify as tax exempt. The costs of the plan are not deductible until the deferred compensation is paid out or becomes nonforfeitable. At death the present value of the deferred benefits becomes taxable to the employee's estate without the estate necessarily having the cash to pay the tax.

Notwithstanding all of this it is possible to have a forfeitable salary continuance, or deferred compensation plan, where the funding is done through purchasing insurance on the life of the participants. The tax-free proceeds of the insurance on the life of the executives who die provide enough profit to the corporation to repay the cost of the insurance and to pay for the cost of the salary continuance.

This plan is not valid for employees of states, municipalities, or tax exempt organizations (October 1978) but are real plums for executives of private corporations.

Summary

A very carefully thought out employee benefit plan is probably the soundest tax shelter left in our law today and a vital ingredient in the financial planning of all working people without regard to their level of compensation. Study this chapter carefully. If you work for a large corporation, review the benefit payment it has given you. Discuss this not only within the corporation but with your own financial advisers and see how your plan compares with the plans of other companies and with other types of capital-generating procedures.

DANGERS OF DOUBLE DOMICILE

These pointers are not for every reader of this book: they are for people who retire from one state to another but still retain some roots in their original home.

Let us suppose a couple has spent their entire life in Pennsylvania and then purchase a condominium in California. Initially they go to their Sun Belt home only for the coldest months, but eventually they find that they are spending more and more time in California, but still returning to Pennsylvania for the summer months.

Suppose the husband then dies and his executor finds that both California and Pennsylvania *each* claim that it was the sole domicile of the deceased husband. The result would be that state inheritance taxes would have to be paid to both Pennsylvania and California.

As a matter of fact, the embattled estate of Howard Hughes had to go to the U.S. Supreme Court because both Texas and California ruled that Hughes had died an exclusive resident of that state.

How can a person be held to live principally in two different states at the same time? Logically this is not possible, but practically, it occurs all too often. The estate of Dr. Dorrance, founder of Campbell Soup, who lived in Camden, New Jersey most of his life and built a retirement home in Pennsylvania, had to pay twenty million dollars in inheritance tax to Pennsylvania and nineteen million to New Jersey.

Accordingly, if you make this kind of move (and increasing numbers of you will do so) ask a tax lawyer how to avoid this double tax. One way of doing it is to give up all assets such as bank accounts, real estate, summer homes, and the like in the old state. If you still want to enjoy your summer home, put it into a trust for your children, reserving the rights of use under it. In this way you will not have to go through probate in the original state. Sun-worshipers beware.

11
Marriage

ARE YOU MARRIED OR NOT?

It need hardly be said that marriage has an enormous romantic, personal effect on women. But the financial impact of marriage is also of the most critical significance.

First of all, what constitutes marriage? A good many women may think that they are single where, in fact, they may be "married" in the eyes of the law. Conversely, some women may think they are married when, in fact, in the eyes of the law they are "single."

Many years ago, a great many states recognized a marital relationship under the name of "common-law marriage." Under this legal doctrine, if a man and a woman (neither of whom was married to someone else) cohabited and held themselves out as husband and wife, the courts determined that this had the same effect as a "ceremonial marriage" before a clergyman or a justice of the peace. The courts differed as to the length of time required to achieve "common-law marriage," but in some states just registering as Mr. & Mrs. John Doe and staying at a hotel overnight was enough to constitute a "common-law marriage."

So many men found themselves caught in this "trap" that by the middle of the century, male-dominated state legislatures had outlawed "common-law marriage."

But by the late seventies, so many couples were living together without benefit of a ceremonial marriage, but with all the other aspects of a marital relationship, that the courts began holding that a "quasimarital relationship" existed. The pendulum then began swinging back again in the direction of "common-law marriage" under its new name of "quasimarriage," so that in fairly short order many women who thought they were single, in fact, were married. (*Quasi* is defined in the dictionary as: "as if, as it were, approximately.")

In one of the most important cases, a famous movie actor was held to have been in a state of quasimarriage after living with a young woman for more than five years. A court determined that a quasi-marital relationship existed and awarded the "wife" one half of the community property, i.e., one half of what had been earned by her quasihusband during the continuance of the relationship. While the development of this doctrine might seem to be entirely favorable for women, it might have disastrous effects as well.

We will discuss some of the favorable aspects of marriage and some of the unfavorable ones, but a quasimarriage has a whole series of special traps of its own that many women should consider before entering into an open, extended cohabitation with a male.

First of all, in the community property states (see chapter on community property), it should be kept in mind that the combination of quasimarriage and community property may cost the woman a fortune. If the quasiwife earned more than her quasihusband, she may discover when the relationship ends that a large amount of her own savings attributable to her earnings during the relationship may be ordered paid over to the husband.

Secondly, she may discover that Uncle Sam will hold her liable for the tax on her quasihusband's earnings, even though she never saw a penny of them. This is discussed at length in the chapter on divorce.

Thirdly, if you have been previously married and divorced, you may discover that under the terms of the divorce settlement this new relationship may terminate your right to alimony. In fact, even without such a provision, there are many states where the law provides that regardless of the presence or absence of any such stipulation in the divorce agreement, that open, "notorious," and continuing cohabitation terminates the obligation for alimony of a prior husband. Any divorced woman receiving alimony should check with her attorney regarding this (see chapter 14, "Selecting Your Financial Professional Advisor," where the selection of a divorce attorney is discussed).

Fourthly, you may go into a ceremonial marriage only to discover that your supposed husband had previously cohabited, under circumstances which constituted a quasimarriage, and that, accordingly, his marriage to you was bigamous and void.

So, look before you leap (into bed)!

Is Your Prospective Husband Financially "Mr. Right"?

You may be so infatuated that you are prepared to marry your beloved even if he has two heads. On the other hand, you may be a hardheaded executive-type lady with enough objectivity to check things out before you say "I do." You are more likely to find yourself in this more cautious category if you have had a previous marital disaster that ended in divorce.

More is involved than just a financial check out. Your man may turn out to be a billionaire with an unblemished financial record, but you may still discover that he is a psychotic, who will make you utterly miserable. But this chapter does not pretend to deal with the psychological traps in marriage, only with the financial ones.

We also realize that some of the information we suggest is important just cannot be obtained, or that you may feel the inquiry is so unromantic that you just have to close your eyes and go ahead with financial blindfolds. But here are some of the facts that you might very well be able to uncover through direct inquiry, or you might have to turn to some lawyer, bank, credit agency, or even a private detective to get the facts. If you have a father or mother living, let him or her do the investigating, and then if the fact of investigation leaks out, you can always blame it on the overzealousness of a loving parent. Here are some of the things to look for.

1. *Has he been married previously, and if so, has the marriage ended in divorce?*

This is one of the most difficult things to check out, since ardent men frequently will lie about this, and you can't check the whole world to discover whether or not he went through a marriage ceremony in Yugoslavia while on a vacation there fifteen years ago. However, there are some ways which offer promise of getting this information quite accurately and very confidentially. A credit checking organization or a private investigator may have access to financial statements, loan applications, and the like. Although social security records are supposed to be superconfidential, we have encountered instances where even access to them can be achieved. Also, if you find out where your beloved has lived over the past few years, a check with the town clerk or county clerk can reveal whether or not a residence was owned by him jointly with a wife.

2. *If he has been married, does he have a heavy load of alimony or child support?*

   If so, you may find that your budget never will be balanced. If your man admits a prior marriage, it seems perfectly appropriate to ask to see the separation or divorce agreement.

3. *Are there any lawsuits pending against him, or are there any unpaid judgments?*

   Of course, you both may be living in California, but he may have a lawsuit pending against him in the State of Maine without having set foot in Maine. You can't discover everything, but you can at least check the facts in any jurisdiction where he has lived.

4. *If he is in business for himself as an individual businessman, or professional, or if he is in a small partnership, or if he is the owner of stock in a corporation with only a few shareholders, what is the credit record of your beloved, individually or as a partner, or what is the credit record of his corporation?*

   If he works for a large corporation, ask your stockbroker, attorney, accountant, or investment advisor, to check on the financial condition and record of the corporation. You may find that you are about to marry a man who has a good, large-paying job with a corporation that is ready to go into bankruptcy, leaving you for a long or short time with a husband who cannot contribute to the support of the household. It is a good idea also to inquire innocently for the length of time he has been with the employer. Some marriages are with a husband who traditionally jumps from job to job with all kinds of family and financial upsets. You might also check whether the corporation which employs him is notorious for moving its executives around all over the world. In Weston, Connecticut, where we live, there are so many executives of this type that a child who has been in the Weston school system for five years is an "old timer."

Such mobility can have disastrous financial results for *you* if *you* are in a job that isn't very portable.

5. *What fringe benefits go with your man's job?*

With many companies, the fringe benefits extend only to the employee and not to his spouse or children. Other companies are much more generous. This is particularly important with regard to health, disability, and life insurance, as previously discussed.

6. *How much life insurance does your prospective husband own personally, and is he ready to assign the policy to you, make you the beneficiary, or better yet, transfer the policy to a trust for the benefit of yourself and your children?*

In the chapters dealing with life insurance and with trusts, we explain the advantage of having insurance held by a trust for your benefit rather than by you personally and rather than by your husband. These questions are also important because it is surprising in how many cases a man is divorced and then remarries and forgets that his first wife was the beneficiary of an insurance policy and forgets to make a change of beneficiary. At the very least this should be checked out.

In other cases, a bachelor has taken out insurance for the benefit of his parents who later die, and then he gets married without making a change of beneficiary.

So, check out the insurance situation at

whatever early date you personally consider appropriate.

7. *How is the health of your fiancé?*

It is obviously romantically impractical to ask your fiancé to spend a week at the Mayo Clinic being checked out, but if there are obvious signs of ill health, give a thought to your situation if you were left widowed at an early age or, worse yet, if your husband comes down with a disability that precludes him from earning a living. One way to approach this is to suggest that you each take out disability policies on the other. In the process of applying for them, you will find out a good deal about the health impairment situation. The same applies if each of you takes out life insurance for the benefit of the other before marriage.

Some Legal Aspects of Marriage

If you and your husband are going to be living in any of the community property states, that is, Arizona, California, Idaho, Louisiana, Nevada, New Mexico, Texas, and Washington, you should keep in mind that you will be the owner of one half of what he earns during your marriage, but also that he would be the owner of one half of what you earn during the marriage. This can be a two-edged sword. We suggest you read the chapter on community property if residence in any of the aforesaid states is involved.

You should also find out what effect marriage will have on your right to make a will benefiting whomever you might choose. In a great many states, a husband or wife *MUST* leave a certain portion of his or her estate to a surviving spouse. This is discussed in detail in chapter 9, "Inheriting It". The laws in many countries, other than the United States, vary widely and may be applicable to your estate or that of your husband if you reside there, whether or not you are a citizen. If you are a person who has considerable wealth, or expects to earn or inherit some, check with your lawyer about a premarital agreement. This is an agreement made before marriage in which the husband and wife surrender the right to dictate how much of an estate must be left to the survivor. But remember, these agreements are among the most difficult to draw up and defend. If either spouse misrepresents his or her wealth to the other, or if either spouse does not have truly "independent counsel" (that is, one not related to the other spouse or having any partnership or similar relationship with the attorney for the other spouse), the agreement becomes void. Many premarital agreements have been set aside because they were not properly drawn or executed.

The various states differ as to the obligation of a husband to support a wife. Some years ago, the states were practically unanimous in requiring that a husband support his wife, except in rare instances where he obtained a divorce for cause (such as adultery). This tradition is gradually withering away, but it still persists, and it would be well for you to find out the law within the jurisdiction where you live.

Be careful about joint ownership of real estate, bank accounts, stockbrokerage accounts, joint safe deposit boxes, or any other property. In many states where there is joint ownership, the survivor takes all, and this may not be what you wish.

One disadvantage of a joint bank account is that your mate can sneak down to the bank and clean you out in anticipation of deserting you or divorcing you. Of course, this works both ways, and you may be able to clean out the bank account if you get there first.

A more serious difficulty of jointly held property is treated in the discussion of the tax consequences of marriage. Usually, it is better to have property owned as "tenants in common" or as separate property. With jointly held property the survivor takes all, and the first person to die is taxed on the entire property, except to the extent that the survivor proves she contributed her *OWN* money to the purchase. With the other two types of holdings, the survivor inherits just her share plus any interest in the husband's which passed to her under his will, intestacy, or community property. But even apart from taxes, tenants in common is usually a neater and more businesslike way of handling your assets.

As a matter of fact, it is very advisable at the time of marriage to list what assets (including furniture and objects of art) are being brought to the marriage by each of the parties. This can avoid a lot of difficulty if, as with 50 percent of marriages, divorce occurs and, from a tax point of view, at death, which occurs in 100 percent of all marriages.

It is well to consult an attorney in the jurisdiction where you live, or are going to live, about the special legal aspects of marriage in that jurisdiction. Usually, you will get some surprises, and the best way of keeping them from being unpleasant surprises is to know about them before you get married.

Once you are married and have made your list of separate assets, you update it with the assistance of your accountant at least once a year.

Also, in the community property states, you should have an annual restatement of what property owned by either husband or wife is community property and what property is separate property. Otherwise, the wife may discover that because he inherited it, or was given it, or earned it before their marriage, or because she agreed to it, it was separate property and she had no community property rights in separate property.

Tax Aspects of Marriage

There are so many tax consequences of marriage that it would take a book four times as large as this entire volume to describe them all. We shall only touch on some of the highlights.

We suggest that before your marriage you consult a tax expert about your specific tax situation and have him or her carefully explain to you the tax facts of marriage.

Here are some of the more important ones.

1. In the community property states (see chapter on this subject), one half of what your husband earns during your marriage belongs to you, without his being subject to a gift tax on it.

2. One spouse can leave one half of his or her "adjusted gross estate" (Your accountant will have to figure this one out, since it is a technical term, namely, total estate minus funeral expenses, administration expenses, debts of decedent, mortgages and liens, net losses during administration, expenses incurred in administering property not subject to claims) to the surviving spouse and avoid estate tax on this. This is known as the "marital deduction" and is further elucidated in chapter 9, "Inheriting It." To qualify for the marital deduction, the bequest must strictly comply with intricate rules of the Internal Revenue Code.

    As of the date of the publication of this book, a spouse can take a marital deduction of $250,000, even if that is more than one half of his adjusted gross estate. In estate planning, it is not always wise to take the full marital deduction if the surviving spouse has extensive means of her own. This depends largely on the relative age of husband and wife and state of health. Even if taking the full marital deduction will eventually build up a larger aggregate estate tax at the death of the surviving wife, if that wife is much younger or much healthier than her husband, the use of the money saved at the death of the husband may justify the ultimate greater aggregate tax. This can be determined only under the special circumstances of each case and only by a very competent estate planner.

3. One spouse can give the other spouse $100,-000 free of gift tax during his lifetime.

4. If a gift is made in the proper fashion to a spouse, only one half of that gift is taxed. This is the "gift tax marital deduction."

5. Husband and wife may join in making gifts or in filing gift tax returns, and the gift tax is then computed as if each spouse had made one half of the gift separately. With the wife's consent, the husband, for example, can make a gift of $6,000 to any donee and the gift will be treated as two gifts of $3,000 each and, therefore, is not taxable.

6. Husband and wife may join in making a joint income tax return. At the higher brackets, this works out enormous income tax savings. This is discussed later in this chapter, and also in part in our chapter on divorce.

7. There is no tax saving in joint ownership of property. The first spouse to die is determined to be taxable on the entire value of the jointly owned property unless the surviving spouse can prove that she contributed to the purchase or acquisition of the jointly owned property with her own funds, *not derived from gifts from her husband* (and vice-versa if the wife dies first). It is extremely hard to demonstrate where the money to buy your home in which you lived for thirty years came from and that the wife's contribution came from sources independent of her husband. Accordingly, it is very dangerous from a tax point of view to hold any property jointly. If

your husband made you an outright gift of an $18,000 diamond engagement ring, but you keep it in a jointly controlled safe deposit box, you may find that it is still taxed as part of his estate. (This is one of the reasons it is better to have separate safe deposit boxes.) The same applies to bearer bonds kept in a joint safe deposit box.

In some states, particularly with estates of under $500,000 (including insurance) it is appropriate to keep a home in joint ownership because the convenience of this and the avoidance of probate expenses may outweigh the tax disadvantages.

There are a host of tax disadvantages to marriage. We mention only a few.

1. If you are deserted and your husband lives in a community property state, you will be subject to income tax on one half of his earnings regardless of whether or not you ever lay your hands on them. This is discussed in the chapter on divorce at great length.

2. The law says (Internal Revenue Code 1348) that *earned income* may not be taxed at more than 50 percent. As of the publication of this book, a single person exceeds the 50 percent bracket over $41,500 and a married one, filing jointly, exceeds it at $60,000 (including spouse's income). However, married persons may *not take advantage of this limitation if they do not file joint returns*.

3. There are two kinds of deductions from a taxable income before you start totaling up. One is called "itemized" deductions. They include many things, such as charitable contributions, medical expenses (under certain limitations), interest (under certain limitations), and so

on. In an effort to simplify the income tax return, the Congress provided for another type of deduction. Here, the deduction is not itemized but is an arbitrary amount that you don't have to back up. This is called the "standard" deduction. For those whose itemized deductions are less than the standard deduction, it is obviously better to take the standard deduction. Moreover, the trend of the law is toward increasing the standard deduction. Here is where marriage can hurt. If you are married (or a surviving spouse with dependents living with you for two years after the death of the husband), you and your husband between you have a standard deduction as of this writing of $3,400. If you are married but choose to file a separate return, you can take $1,700 and presumably your spouse may also take $1,700. But, in the case of an individual who is not married and is not a "surviving spouse" (see two-year rule mentioned above), you and your man can each take a standard deduction of $2,300, or $4,600 between you. As soon as you get married, the two of you, instead of being able to take $4,600 of standard deductions, are limited to $3,400 (IRC Section 141). So, you see, it costs the tax on $1,200 to get married provided that your itemized deductions are not in excess of $4,600.

4. If you own stock or some other capital asset that is now worth less than what you paid for it, you can sell it and take a capital loss, but if you sell it to your spouse the loss is disallowed.

5. Separate corporations each pay a graduated tax hitting the maximum 46 percent at $100,-000 of taxable corporate income. If Jane Doe owns Corporation A making $50,000,

and Robert Roe owns Corporation B making $50,000, the two corporations between them pay only $18,500 in taxes on $100,000 of income. But let Robert and Jane become married and then the ownership of stock is "attributed" to each other. Corporations A and B are taxed as if they were one corporation. For the stockholders of Corporations A and B to marry is going to cost the two corporations between them $8,250 more in tax on an aggregate income of $100,000.

All kinds of other unhappy events can come from this attribution rule. We shall mention only a few.

If Corporation A, as above, is not commonly controlled with B, and A has only one employee (for example, an incorporated inventor), he can install a very juicy pension plan for the benefit of the inventor. In the meantime, if Corporation B has 200 employees, the sole stockholder would probably shrink from having a pension plan as lucrative as that offered by Corporation A. In Corporation A, the stockholder gets 100 percent of the benefits. But once the owners of A and B get married, they become commonly controlled and one corporation may not furnish a less favorable pension than the other.

The government taxes corporations which have unreasonably large surpluses, but the law provides that the size of the surplus is not considered until the accumulated earnings exceed $150,000. As long as the owners of Corporations A and B are not married, each corporation may accumulate $150,000 without concern about accumulation of surplus tax. The moment the owners become married these corporations are "commonly controlled" and the exemption applies not to $300,000

(A's \$150,000 + B's \$150,000) but only to
\$150,000 as between the corporations.

7. If you sell *part* of your stock in one corporation which you control, the sales price may be
taxed to you, not as a capital gain, but at a
much higher rate, as ordinary income. But
suppose you sell *all* of your stock back to the
parent corporation, but your husband retains
part of his stock? Then your husband's stock
will be "attributed" to you and you will not
be deemed to have sold *all* of your stock
back to the corporation and will be hit (unless you come within certain very technical
limitations) with the ordinary income tax
rather than the capital gains tax. *Note:* The
reason for selling your stock back to a corporation which you control is to get money
out of the corporation in a form that will not
be considered a dividend. Dividends would
be taxed at a far higher rate than the proceeds of a stock sale, at capital gain rates.

8. If Jane and John both work for a big corporation which pays John a high salary and
Jane a much lower salary, and Jane and John
get married, then their aggregate tax will be
sharply reduced (see Joint Tax Returns).

9. On the other hand, if Richard and Mary, who
have founded an advertising agency, each
owning one half of the stock, decide to get
married, Mary may decide to sell her stock
back to the corporation and use the proceeds
to purchase a beautiful home. In this case, it
is essential that Mary make the sale prior to
marriage. If she waits for the wedding bells,
her gain would be taxed as ordinary income,
unless she satisfied some very restrictive conditions in the tax law. The best procedure for
Mary is for her to sell the stock before the
marriage but be paid out in installments

mostly after the marriage, in which case Mary would not only get capital gain treatment but also the capital gain would be taxed at a lower level because it would be reported on a joint tax return. This would reduce the tax by as much as 75 percent.

10. If a husband lends money to his wife and she loses the money in a business enterprise, she is precluded from taking an ordinary business deductible loss. This can be avoided by the husband and wife forming a family partnership.

11. Corporations with passive income, or income earned by the owner of more than 25 percent of the stock, are subject to a special penalty tax known as the "personal holding company tax," provided that the corporation is controlled by not more than five people.

The trouble with marriage here is that a husband and wife are treated as one person in tallying up the count of five individuals.

There are a great many other situations where marriage has a major effect, either good or bad, on your tax situation, but we cannot begin to enumerate them all. Before getting married, you should review your situation with a competent tax adviser and see whether marriage will have a favorable or unfavorable tax effect. If the net effect is unfavorable, this does not mean that you should not get married, but it does mean that before your marriage, it might be a good idea to take certain protective action so as to minimize or eliminate the adverse effect of marriage.

The foregoing comments were as of the date of the writing of this book. Tax laws are constantly changing, however, and we recommend that you treat the foregoing as only examples of how the income tax law worked in early 1979. By the time you pick up this book, the law may have been expanded or liberalized.

This is another reason why this chapter (as with most of the others) should be treated merely as a collation of symptoms which should lead you to seek professional help. (See chapter 14.)

JOINT TAX RETURNS

On or about April 15, the words, "Sign here, dear" echo through the land in all joint tax return states. Agreeable wives (or husbands) obediently sign, hardly reading the return, and practically never receiving a copy. Yet the signature adds hundreds of dollars of spendable income. How much depends on the joint income? For a couple earning jointly around $32,000 the signature of a spouse can mean $7,100 (see chart, p. 220).

Joint returns were voted in by Congress in 1948 so that a married couple could compute its tax as if each spouse had earned half of the income. This was intended to put noncommunity property states in a position of tax equality with community property states (see chapter 13, "Community Property"). The advantages of this procedure are give a dollar value at 1977 rates in the chart on p. 220.

That is the positive side. On the negative side, should one spouse go broke, or disappear, or make fraudulent statements, the other spouse is equally liable for the tax consequences. When the Internal Revenue Service says you owe a bundle, and your other half has vanished, and you say, "But, but, but, I didn't earn anything that year," the answer will be, "But you signed the return, and *you* have to pay."

Should your other (not better) half make fraudulent statements, you have to prove you didn't know about the fraud if you want to escape the penalties. The logic seems to be that if you enjoy the tax benefits of a joint return, you also have to share in the penalties if things go wrong.

In the case of the death of a spouse, the survivor

can continue to file a joint return for two consecutive taxable years if he or she maintains a household with dependents living there. The survivor can also take advantage of head-of-household brackets. This eases the financial impact of death but hardly goes far enough to compensate for the decline of income and increase of expenses that frequently happen in such a loss.

Whatever the marital situation may be, when that second signature goes on the joint tax return, it should light up in dollar signs showing the value of a spouse to a taxpayer, as determined by Congress when it wrote the tax law.

As we will discuss in chapter 12, "Divorce," joint returns can be very helpful in the case of a marital rift. The wife who signed them can get back returns for many years and thus help her attorney and accountant discover hidden income and hidden wealth. Also, unless the parties live in a community property state, the wife can deny her husband the tax savings of joint returns by simply refusing to sign a joint return. This will vastly increase his tax and the amount of income he has to earn just to have the same after-tax income as he had when the wife was signing joint returns. Thus, a husband earning $32,000 a year will have to earn $7,100 more a year just to remain even if his wife refuses to sign a joint return. As the income climbs, so the blow climbs and becomes heavier, as illustrated in column E of the chart on p. 220.

Finally, if a married man does not file a joint return, the 50 percent ceiling of tax on *earned* income will no longer protect him and his tax can be increased by as much as 40 percent (the maximum rate can go from 50 to 70 percent). While these exact figures may change with future changes in tax rates and the tax law, this is a tactic that estranged wives should know about. Of course, where the woman is the big money-maker, the husband can use these tactics too.

CHART
(Pre 1979 Rates)

A	B	C	D	E
Net Taxable Income	Tax— Joint Return	Disposable Income	Increased Income Needed (rounded)*	Tax Value of Spouse (D) − (A)
20,000	4,380	15,620	23,300	3,300
32,000	8,660	23,340	39,100	7,100
44,000	14,060	29,940	57,000	13,000
52,000	18,060	33,940	68,000	16,000
64,000	24,420	39,580	84,500	20,500
76,000	31,020	44,980	101,000	25,000
88,000	37,980	50,120	120,000	32,000
100,000	45,180	54,820	133,000	33,000
200,000	89,020	110,980	320,000	120,000

* Increased Income Needed Without Joint Return To Produce Sums In Column C

12
Divorce

Divorce is one of the most climactic events in the life and the financial planning of a woman, and it is frequently the worst handled.

In 1964 one of your authors published a book on financial planning for women, *What Every Woman Doesn't Know*. It had a chapter on divorce. For a decade and a half the author has been deluged with phone calls, letters, and even unannounced personal visits from a huge number of either about-to-be divorced ladies or those who had already been divorced. One pathetic woman wrote in and stated that she had been referred to this book and had gone to the Seattle public library to get the book and read the chapter, only to find that the chapter had been torn out of the book. We never discovered whether the miscreant was a greedy wife who didn't want to purchase the book (now out of print) or some cagey husband who didn't want to have his wife obtain the benefits of reading the chapter.

Unfortunately, a clear predominance of these women

have been persons who had *already signed a divorce
agreement or completed divorce proceedings*. In some
particularly outrageous situations, especially when not
too much time had passed, it was possible to improve
the deal the woman had received, but in most instances
it was too late.

There are two major hazards that a woman faces
with divorce encounters. The first of these is her own
emotional situation. The second, we are sorry to say, is
the gross ineptitude or carelessness of her legal representation.

The emotional problems of women involved in divorce break down into three major categories.

The first of these is where the wife takes the initiative
in wanting the divorce. The second is where the husband walks out on the wife. The third is where both of
them get sick of each other more or less simultaneously.

Where the wife wants out, there is a grave danger
that she will be so anxious to get rid of her husband
that she will sacrifice all kinds of rights which she would
otherwise enjoy. This is particularly so where there is
another man. In such situations women not only sacrifice adequate provisions for their own support but accept grossly inadequate provisions for child support.

Moreover, all too often, where a wife settles for pea-
nuts because she has fallen in love with some other
man, the other man disappears—sometimes even before the formulation of divorce can be completed
—and the wife is stuck.

We have seen hundreds and hundreds of cases of
this kind. In one situation, the wife accepted a settlement of $10,000 a year, not knowing that her husband
was earning over $100,000 a year. By the time the
divorce was granted, the "other man" had disappeared.
But when the wife tried to reopen the divorce settlement, she was held, after three years of litigation, to
be stuck with the settlement. This happens over and
over again.

In the second category, the wife is so stunned by

her husband's rejection of her that she just wants to get out of the horrible situation as fast as she can, and at any price. Here, too, when the dust settles, the wife will often bitterly regret the inadequacy of her settlement, but it will be too late to alter it.

In the third category, both people will want to rush things and frequently engage the same lawyer "friend of the family" to act as mediator between them. We shall discuss this further when speaking about the role of attorneys in divorce. At this point, we'll say that after experiences with scores and scores of such divorce settlements, we have found that more often than not the "friend of the family" turns out to be more friendly to the husband than to the wife.

What to do about it? The first thing to keep in mind is that if you are divorced locally the procedure will usually take five to ten times as long as you expected. (As you will see, getting a "quickie" divorce in places like Santo Domingo is not at all to be recommended.)

What usually happens is that a separation agreement is negotiated and executed and then later the divorce court approves and confirms the agreement. Between these steps is a vast quagmire of legal red tape. Many states require "reconciliation counseling" as a prelude to a divorce. Although we have hardly ever observed such reconciliation counseling to be effective, it invariably delays the legal conclusion of a settlement agreement often hastily entered into months before.

Accordingly, when divorce looms on the horizon, no matter what the circumstances, the best thing for the woman to do is to recover her emotional equilibrium and poise by going off on a long holiday, either by herself or with some woman friend.

Then when she returns she should seriously consider some psychological counseling. Sometimes this may take the form of joint sessions between husband and wife or even family groups including the children (or at least the older ones) with some psychologist or psychiatrist. This is far different from most reconciliation efforts by a court-appointed counsel who may not even have had advance psychiatric or psychological training or qualifications.

Whether or not this will "save" the marriage, it will at least serve to achieve emotional stability for the wife, possibly avoid extreme bitterness between the husband and wife, and usually be vastly helpful for the children. It will help the wife go into the divorce negotiations and legal proceedings in a healthier fashion and always with better financial results.

By better financial results, we do not necessarily mean the payment of larger sums for longer periods. Extortion by a bitter wife, even if financially gratifying, can be emotionally devastating. We have seen women who lived out their lives in bitter loneliness rather than let their ex-husbands off the hook of paying alimony by remarrying. Frequently, the best form of settlement will be for the husband to pay the wife larger installments for a few years, or up to as long as ten years, whether or not she remarries. This has two advantages: In the first place, it will permit the wife to become rehabilitated and be paid for her years of servitude, regardless of when she remarries. (This is not so important in community property states where the wife is usually "compensated" for this service by receiving one half of what her husband's earnings accumulate during the marriage.) (See chapter 13, "Community Property.")

The second advantage of payment installments not exceeding ten years is that such payments are *not taxable to the wife*. They are also not tax deductible for the husband. If the payments are to continue for more than ten years, that becomes "alimony" instead of installment payments and becomes *tax deductible to the husband and taxable to the wife.* Watch out for settlements which provide for 121 monthly payments. That last month, going beyond a ten-year period, makes the entire amount taxable to the wife, beginning with the very first payment.

If the wife keeps these recommendations in mind, she should then be able to enter into negotiations with a clear head. But she still needs a highly proficient attorney to adequately protect her interests.

THE ATTORNEY

Of all the fields in which unskilled or improperly motivated attorneys do damage, the field of divorce is one of the two leaders. The other field is estate planning (see chapter 9, "Inheriting It").

We recently observed one case where the wife went to very competent counsel. But they were competent in the field of corporate law, SEC matters, and probate. They were not competent in the area of divorce and they really didn't have any taste for this type of matter. The result was that her husband, who had recently inherited three million dollars and who had elected to discard his wife for a young woman, was obligated to pay the rejected wife only $27,000 for one year and $20,000 for two more years and then nothing, although the wife had no earning experience and had been married for many years.

One grave danger of inadequate divorce settlements is that even if the wife gets custody of the children, if the husband is financially in a much stronger position, he will be able to "bribe" the children and win away their allegiance from their mother. If there is not proper provision for summer camp, prep school, or college education to be paid for by the wife out of child support payments made to her, the husband can frequently step in, select the camp and schools, pay for them, and thus gain the gratitude and allegiance of the children. Incidentally, child support payments are not taxable to the mother and not tax deductible for the husband. (It is important that the separation agreement provide which spouse will be entitled to claim the very important tax exemption for minor children.)

Remember, once the separation agreement has been

signed it is almost impossible to open it up again and practically impossible to disturb it once a court has confirmed the agreement in a divorce decree. Sometimes it is very useful to have provisions in a divorce settlement providing for adjustment of payments either by agreement or by arbitration. Such adjustments may be necessary upward because of cost-of-living circumstances or downward because the husband's earnings sharply decrease or his health deteriorates. Remember, you cannot get blood out of a stone.

The friend of the family who acts as attorney for both sides is almost certain to favor the husband, who is more apt to be a client or potential client of such an attorney than is the wife. Incidentally, this is one situation where a divorce settlement can be opened up, as a rule, because the wife did not have independent legal representation. Another situation where this can be done is where the child support payments are inadequate. An ill-advised wife and mother may *not* bargain away the rights of her children to be adequately supported in the light of the husband's future income and their needs.

Well, how does the wife go about getting a good lawyer? As we have indicated, the most important prelude is to have her regain her emotional stability and poise. The second ingredient is for her to take her time. She will have to wait a long time for the divorce in any case, so she might as well move forward cautiously and intelligently in the selection of an attorney.

Usually, it is a good idea to use a lawyer who either specializes in divorce matters exclusively or who at least has a large portion of his practice in the area of divorce. On the other hand, the divorce practice should not be so very large that you will be lost in the shuffle while the lawyer devotes his attentions primarily to divorce cases which may be more lucrative.

It is frequently very helpful to speak to your divorced friends and find out how they feel about their respective attorneys and their efficiency some years after their own divorce.

It is extremely important that a fair fee be paid. If the fee is inadequate, the attorney, unfortunately, may find himself engrossed in other, more financially rewarding cases and neglect your matter. It is usually worthwhile to arrange for a larger fee if the case goes to trial than if it is settled. If the fee is determined without regard to settlement or trial, the lawyer will be tempted to settle quickly in order to get the same amount of money with less work.

On the other hand, the fee for trial should not be too juicy or the lawyer may be tempted to avoid a decent settlement and drag you through a corrosive trial just to earn a highly enhanced fee.

It is absolutely essential that *you* arrange the fee and that *you* pay it. It may well be that your husband will, by agreement or court order, pay you the amount of your legal fees, and you then pay the attorney. But it is essential that *you* will have negotiated the fee. It is just plain murder to have your husband or his lawyer negotiate your lawyer's fee. Frequently, the husbands pay inappropriately large fees which they have negotiated and thus end up with the lawyer really working for the husband rather than for you. In almost all states, if the husband doesn't agree with you about the payment of counsel fee, the court will order him to make the payment to you. But in such cases it will not have been the husband who has determined the fee that your attorney will receive.

The legal fee will not be taxable to you nor deductible by you or your husband. This will not apply to payment for the tax-advice elements in the matter.

Keep in constant touch with your attorney so that your case is not put on a back burner. At the same time, do not "bug" your lawyer with daily telephone calls. It is essential that you strike an effective balance in regard to these matters. (See also chapter 14.)

It is frequently important to have separate tax counsel advising you as to the tax consequences of your divorce settlement.

It is absolutely essential in almost every case that the agreement provide that if the husband defaults in making his payments that the court will also award you the amount of your counsel fee incurred in collecting what is owing to you. Unfortunately, in most matters, the prevailing party has to pay her own lawyer without reimbursement from the husband (except in the initial divorce). Without such provision, some husbands will compel their ex-wives to sue them every month for that month's payment, with the result that most of the wife's money and emotional capital will go down the drain. This is of critical importance.

Frequently the wife is advised to get a "quickie" divorce in some foreign jurisdiction such as Santo Domingo. In such cases the wife flies down to Santo Domingo one day, gets a divorce the next day, and then returns. In the first place, such a divorce is not binding unless the husband agrees to it. Even then, the validity of such divorce may be attacked. While some recent cases sustain such divorces where the husband has consented, this has frequently involved lengthy legal controversy, and there may be some situations in which the wife may discover that the divorce was not valid at all. Moreover, it is much harder to enforce a foreign divorce. In many cases where the divorce is a local one and the husband defaults in making alimony payments the court may, and frequently does, hold the husband in "contempt of court" and fine him or even throw him into jail for nonpayment of alimony. This usually cannot be done with a foreign divorce.

More and more woman lawyers are found in the divorce field. Frequently such lawyers are well equipped to represent their woman clients. However, this does not happen automatically. It is still important that the woman attorney have an impressive background of experience and specialization. It is also important that she not convert your divorce case into a battlefield for a women's liberation vendetta which she may be carrying on. This is by no means the case with all woman lawyers, but it is something to watch out for. Correspondingly, if you have a man lawyer, watch out for some unconscious or semiconscious sympathy for the male animal.

The divorce settlement may provide for the mandatory inclusion of your children in your husband's will. If this is the case, particularly if your husband is a wealthy man, such provision should be carefully worded so that your children are not disinherited.

Usually alimony ceases with the death of the husband. Accordingly, you should get substantial life insurance on him, and the alimony payments should be sufficient to allow for the payment of the premiums. Remember, such premium payments are not tax deductible, although the alimony will be taxable to you. Frequently, it is better to have your husband give you already existing policies taken out at a younger age, which will be cheaper and easier for you to continue. Under no circumstances let him retain ownership of the policy.

Consideration should be given to providing for the continuance of his health and medical insurance for your benefit and particularly for that of the children. This is especially important in regard to coverage financed by your husband's employer.

If you have been married for approximately ten years, have your attorney check out your rights with regard to your husband's social security.

Do not rely on an assignment by your husband of all or part of his pension rights under a qualified plan. The 1974 Pension Reform Act especially provides that such pension rights are not assignable. The law is not clear as to the pension rights of a wife in a community property state.

THE DISAPPEARING HUSBAND

If your husband disappears, track him down as quickly as you can. A cold trail is harder to find. This is important not only for the purpose of compelling him to support you and your children, but also to avoid a tax trap we shall describe.

When you locate him, move promptly to terminate the marital relationship. The reason for this is a series of absolutely outrageous cases and one U.S. Supreme Court decision. We are amazed that some woman's organization has not fought for correcting legislation on this point. Let us tell you what happened in one of these cases. As you will see from the chapter on community property, half of what a husband earns in community property states is held to belong to the wife. What happened in this one Supreme Court case is that this woman lived in Louisiana, a community property state. Her husband disappeared. She did not know where he was. She did not know what he was earning. She did not get any part of these earnings, although she was technically entitled to half of them. The Supreme Court held that notwithstanding this, the wife—not the disappearing husband—had to pay the tax on half of his income, notwithstanding the fact that he had spent it all. To add insult to injury, the wife was subjected to a 25-percent penalty plus interest for not including this unknown income in her tax return.

Even if you live in an eastern or northern state which does not have community property, the same rule applies if a disappearing husband moves into a community property state in the south or west, earns money, spends it all on himself (and probably a girl friend) but pays tax on only half of it. The deserted wife is still responsible for tax on one half of the income. Accordingly, if your husband disappears, move to get a divorce for desertion so that the marital relationship between you is terminated and you are not deemed legally to have received one half of his income, regardless of whether or not you actually got it. This is not the case unless he has moved into a community property state, but if he disappeared, how can you tell where he is? California has a provision negating community property allocation of earnings after a couple has separated. However, the interpretation of this provision is clouded (What is "separation"?), and other community property states do not always have similar provisions. If you know that he has moved into a community property state and has just deserted you rather than disappeared, it's particularly important to move promptly. In such cases what we have said about proceeding leisurely about getting a divorce does not apply. There are exceptions to every rule.

At this point in your thinking on divorce, you should read the chapter on joint tax returns. These are treasure troves in divorce proceedings. You can write to the IRS and get joint returns you and your husband made (and of which you probably never kept copies) for many years back. In the hands of a good tax attorney and accountant, these will disclose sources of income and capital you otherwise might not know about. For example, a deduction for depreciation may reflect the ownership of secretly owned real estate or other tangible property such as an oil well. An item of income for interest may show a large bank account you never knew about.

Also, if you refuse to sign current joint returns, it will threaten your recalcitrant husband with large increases in *his* tax liability. This tends to make him more reasonable in recognizing his obligation to you. The chapter on joint returns can give you an idea of how much this could cost him. The husband may be asking you to help support some other woman by cutting his taxes in filing a joint return. On the other hand, in a divorce settlement, be sure that you are not stuck with personal liability for his taxes, which you may be held for because you signed his return during happier times.

13

Community Property

This is a highly technical, little understood but critically important, part of any kind of financial or estate planning by a woman.

Most of the northeast, southeast, and middle west states were originally settled by English-speaking people who brought English law with them. But in a curve of states stretching from Louisiana to Washington the states were originally settled by Spanish-speaking people, and with them came a provision of family law derived from Spanish legal influences. This is known as community property law.

The community property states are: Arizona, California, Idaho, Louisiana, Nevada, New Mexico, Texas, and Washington.

In the chapter on inheritance we point out the wife's intestate rights (if there is no will) and her "right of election" against her husband's will if she is inadequately provided for. These rules vary from state to state. With a $300,000 estate where there is no will, or an election is made by the widow, a woman who happens to live in Connecticut, and there is one child, will collect at least $175,000, while a woman who happens to live in California will collect $200,000.

In a totally simplified form, community property means that each spouse is deemed to own half of everything the other spouse earned during their period of marriage. There are many modifications and exceptions to this, which we shall mention.

It is a great mistake to think that you are affected by the law of community property only if you are a married woman living in one of the community property states. The law can extend much farther. Suppose your father has married for a second time and moved to California. He knows that the community property law of that state gives his new wife a right to half of his earnings, and feeling that this will not provide adequately for you, he insures his life for your benefit. When your father dies, you will be shocked to learn that through a series of California decisions your stepmother may claim half of the insurance your father intended for you. Furthermore, if she does not claim it she may have to pay a gift tax on the half she might otherwise have claimed. In one case, a GI designated his mother beneficiary of his National Service Life Insurance. When he died his wife tried to claim half of the insurance specified for her mother-in-law. The case had to be taken all the way to the U.S. Supreme Court which finally held that Congress has the constitutional right to supersede the law of California and may rule that life insurance provided by the government can be paid to anyone the insurer designates. But three U.S. Supreme Court justices dissented.

Community property law may not only affect any aspect of property of married couples living in the community property states, but may also affect property entering or leaving those states in the form of bequests, gifts, and even sales and charitable donations.

Here are some basic questions about community property.

What rights has the wife, as opposed to her husband, during his lifetime, and what rights has the husband, as opposed to his wife, during his lifetime?

What happens if either husband or wife transfers property by sale, gift, bequest, or the designation of an insurance beneficiary?

What happens when a couple moves into or out of a community property state?

What are the income tax consequences to a couple in a community property state? The gift tax consequences? The estate tax consequences?

What can a woman do to best protect the interests of herself and her children? What can the husband do to best protect the interests of his children?

Basically, in community property states all property and income of a married couple is presumed to be community property, owned in equal shares by husband and wife. In most states, this is presumed to include even real estate registered in a single name. What is excluded is property which is proved to be "separate property."

Typical separate property is a possession of the husband or wife acquired before marriage or inherited during marriage. As it is frequently difficult to identify separate property, persons about to marry or to move into or out of a community property state should have a detailed listing of their assets, stating clearly what is the separate property of either husband or wife. Such a schedule should be executed in formal accordance with the laws of the particular state. Property can usually be changed from community to separate property or from separate to community property by agreement, but here too, it is important that legal formalities be observed and that you first consider the tax consequences, particularly with regard to life insurance.

While property clearly acquired before marriage remains the separate property of the owner, problems arise when property is acquired partly before and partly after marriage. For example, let us assume that a man buys property subject to a large mortgage, then marries and pays off the mortgage with his earnings during the course of his marriage. It is sometimes held that the property is separate property, but that the wife has a right to remuneration plus interest for half of the community earnings employed to complete the purchase. In other cases it is held that the entire property is community property, but that the husband has a right to be reimbursed for the funds he paid out prior to the marriage. The laws—as well as the circumstances —vary so widely that you must obtain special legal advice as to the rights of yourself and your husband and all the tax consequences of ownership of the property.

Any proceeds of labor, such as salary or wages, become community property if earned during the marriage. However, the statutes of certain states provide that property acquired by a wife through her own labors are not subject to the claims of her husband's creditors, even though it is technically community property.

Workman's compensation awards and employer insurance or other security also are community property. In some cases, the earnings of underage children become community property; a Texas court has even ruled that the earnings of a minor stepchild belong as community property, to the parent and stepparent.

Generally, inherited property belongs separately to the spouse who has inherited it. But if the inheritance is a result of labor and industry on the part of both the husband and wife—for example, if a parent bequeaths property to his son in exchange for care during his old age by the son and daughter-in-law—the property is community property.

Property which is received as a gift is also separate property. However, careful distinction must be made

between an actual gift and remuneration for services
rendered. For example, a "gift" of stock from a major
stockholder of a corporation to an employee, as a reward for services rendered, will generally be treated
both as compensation, for tax purposes, and as "earned"
property, for community property purposes. It is not
always easy to draw the line, and these matters must
often be decided on a separate appraisal of the facts.

When separate property earns income, the income is
also generally considered separate property. This is a
variation from the old Spanish rule, still followed in
Idaho, Texas, and Louisiana, which states that even
earnings of separate property become part of the community property during marriage. But again, a distinction has to be made between earned and unearned
increment. Suppose a husband inherits a business and
builds it up during his marriage. To what extent is the
increased value of the business as a result of his services
part of the community property and to what extent is
it merely the result of a natural increase in value of
the original separate property? This has always been a
thorny problem. In some states, earnings equivalent to
a salary are treated as community property and the
balance as separate property. In other instances, the
division is reversed; separate property is allowed an
increase in value equal to a normal rate of interest,
with everything else considered a result of services of
the husband, and thus part of the community property.

If separate property is sold and the proceeds are used
to buy other property, the replacement remains separate property unless the original owner chooses to make
it community property. Similarly, if property is bought
on credit, with separate property pledged as collateral,
the new property remains separate. On the other hand,
when personal credit without collateral is used, property acquired with borrowed funds during marriage is
usually deemed to be community property.

Even in Spain in the fifteenth century, when values
remained comparatively stable, it was difficult to desig-

nate a given asset of mixed origin as being either separate or community property. But in the economy of the United States today, the problem is many times greater, for the proceeds of property may be highly disproportionate to its cost. For example, suppose a young bachelor insures his life for $100,000 and pays one premium of $2,000. He then marries and out of his community property earnings pays a second premium of $2,000. Then he dies. If the proceeds of the payments—made half before marriage and half after—were only $4,000 plus interest, the allocation would be relatively simple. But here we have $100,000. Insurance laws in particular vary from state to state. In California, the proceeds of insurance are treated as community property in proportion to the premiums paid. In the example, since one half of the premiums were paid during marriage, one half of the proceeds would be community property.

Of course, when insurance is taken out during the marriage and paid for out of community property, the proceeds are community property. Suppose the beneficiary is a third party? The problem now arises of whether the husband can give away community property. (This we shall discuss later.) In some community property states, if during marriage a man takes out an insurance policy which names his wife as beneficiary and which is paid for by community property funds, and he, the insured, does not reserve the right to change the beneficiary, the wife is simply deemed sole owner of the proceeds as her separate property.

It is impossible, with the great variations among states, to give a generalized answer to the question of whether or not the proceeds of a damage claim for personal injuries belongs to the couple as community property. We can merely recommend that if an accident occurs, great care should be taken that the claim is properly processed to cover the interest of both husband and wife. This is particularly important if negligence on the part of either husband or wife had had anything to do with the accident. In many of the states which do not adhere to the community property law, a wife has the right to sue for injuries suffered through the negligence of her husband, and even to collect on her husband's insurance policy.

We have already mentioned that when a couple moves into or out of a community property state, the move may have a vital effect on the ownership of their property or the proceeds of their earnings. Usually, property acquired in one state as separate property retains its classification when the parties move to a community property state. However, it does not always work out so simply. An insurance policy taken out in New York becomes subject to community property laws if you move to California and pay premiums while living there. Thus, when moves between states are made, it is particularly important to reexamine the insurance program and the wills of both yourself and your husband and to list carefully any property owned separately. This becomes especially complicated for executives who are shifted regularly between New York or other East Coast states and California, Washington, or the southwestern states.

Moreover, there is a new principle found, for example, in California. This is quasicommunity property. Under this doctrine, if a husband has acquired, during the marriage, personal property (anything other than real estate) in a non-community property state, and then moves into California, the property may become community property, if it would have been community property if the couple had lived in California at the time it was acquired.

However, this doctrine is terribly complicated without too many precedents to help us. In some instances, the property earned outside of California does become community property when the couple moves to California, and in other instances it does not. Thus, in some instances, property acquired before residence in California, which would have been community property had the couple lived in California at that time, becomes community property on moving into the state.

It is thus of the utmost importance to consult counsel in both your old state and your new state whenever you move from a non-community property state to a community property state, or from the community property state into a non-community property state, or from one community property state to another community property state, because community property law may be different in important respects from that of the former state. *This is absolutely essential.*

So far, we have been discussing primarily the question of whether or not a given asset is community property. Now we come to an even more interesting question, that of the rights of the couple and their heirs or assignees with regard to community property. The right of the wife is that of an owner of half of the community property. The husband is the manager as to what he earned; he may handle the investment of the community property during his life, unless he becomes incapacitated, as long as the marriage lasts. But this does not mean he can give it away or deal with it fraudulently. Before 1927, a misconception of the law in most states limited the rights of the wife to something less than ownership, even beyond the husband's right of management. In 1927, a statutory correction of a judicial mistake determined that the wife has rights to ownership, although property is still subject to the husband's management. Nevertheless, the rights of the wife in that state may be affected by when a given piece of property was acquired.

In most states, for example, if the wife earns money herself, she no longer loses the management of these earnings to her husband, despite the fact that he shares equally in their ownership as community property. Generally, the husband has the exclusive right to make contracts with regard to community property. There are, however, many situations in which the husband's rights are less than those just stated and the wife's are greater. As a matter of administrative precaution and the protection of the rights of third parties, some states require that both husband and wife participate in the execution of documents transferring property, particularly real estate.

For example, the wife must join the conveyance of real estate under the laws of California, Washington, and Arizona. Sometimes, as in Nevada, Oklahoma, Texas, and Louisiana, the joining of the wife in the conveyance is limited to the transfer of their home. In California, you must join with your husband in the transfer of community property if it is real estate, including gas and oil wells, but he can lease the property for a period less than a year without consent. Variations with regard to real estate are so numerous that we suggest you check specific situations with local counsel. Also, the managerial rights of wives are being constantly expanded each year in many states.

Although your husband may consent to your action in the disposition of community property, it is advantageous to have this formally indicated in writing. In one case, a husband informed his wife that he agreed to her sale of the family business, and she entered into an agreement to do so. He was then allowed to prove that the contract was unenforceable because he had withdrawn the authority he had granted his wife. Therefore, in business dealings with a woman in a community property state, be sure that she has authority to act. If you are a community property wife, be sure that you do not get involved in litigation by making contracts with regard to community property without the clear power to do so.

In most states, the law is developed to the point where the husband and wife both have management of the community property as if they were partners. Accordingly, in community property states, the authority of the person who transfers property to you should be carefully checked out by your attorney.

Even where the consent of the wife is necessary to

the transfer of community property, such as real estate, it is a good idea for you to make sure that such community property is recorded in the names of both you and your husband. If this is not done, someone who takes title from your husband alone may be able to hold on to it, unless you act promptly. If property is community property and there is no reason to change it, you should be sure that you are protected in your community property rights as far as possible. This means, at least in the case of real estate, that the property should be recorded in the names of both parties. This works in reverse if property is transferred by the wife.

Neither husband nor wife can make a gift of community property without the consent of the other spouse.

In some states, a wife must join in a lease of real estate for the lease to be valid. It depends on the record title in some cases, on the length of the lease in other cases, and varies from state to state. We can only suggest that if you are going to lease property, such as a home, to someone else in any of the community property states, you should check with your attorney and obtain the signature of both your husband and yourself on the lease as a precaution, unless your lawyer advises you that for some special reason this is not necessary. If you rent from someone else, obtain the signatures of both husband and wife.

We have said before that the husband generally may not make gifts of community property. Of course, this limitation does not apply if the wife consents to the gift, and in some states, such as Texas, Nevada, Arizona, and Louisiana, moderate gifts will be recognized without such consent. In this connection, remember that death changes the situation. For example, if a California man gives away community property, his wife can void the entire gift while he is alive. After his death she can void it to the extent of only half of the gift because the death of one party separates the community property.

The position of a wife whose husband is wasting the community property by dissolute or extravagant living or gambling is sometimes in question. The courts are reluctant to step in and interfere with a man's way of life, except if the losses are very substantial or there is clearly a case of fraud. Of course, you can go into the divorce courts and obtain a divorce or separation with adequate protection of the remaining community property. Your right to recapture community property transferred before divorce or separation is more difficult to establish. But even without divorce, you may well have the right to pursue the other parties if there is extreme extravagance, gambling, or a conspiracy to defeat your rights.

Community property gambled away by the husband may usually be recovered by the wife.

Early in this chapter we discussed the case of the Californian who insured his life in favor of his daughter. Generally, insurance is treated as a gift and is subject to recapture by the wife if community property funds were used to pay the premiums and the beneficiary named was someone other than herself. Some states permit individual action without the consent of the wife if the beneficiary is someone the husband was obligated to support. Other states, such as Washington, do not.

In Louisiana and California, it is possible for a wife to show that the management of the community property by the husband has been so bad as to warrant a dissolution of the community property relationship, even without a termination of the marriage.

If you have income of your own, particularly if it is earned through your own efforts, you should give careful thought to what your rights may be. Even assuming that your husband in no way interferes with your disposition of the funds, there still may be a tax question as to whether he is making a gift to you. In most states, for instance, the wife is allowed to manage her own earnings even though they are community property. If these earning are then used to buy property which is recorded in her own name, it might be considered, depending on the state in which she lives, separate property, or it might be subject to the laws of community property. Moreover, if it becomes her own separate property, it might be held by the federal authorities that her husband has made a gift to her of what otherwise would have been his community property share. It is therefore particularly important for a married woman who earns substantial sums and who lives in a community property state to check with an attorney and a tax adviser both the legal and tax consequences of investing these funds in real estate, securities, or other holdings.

We now come to the awkward question of the liability of the married couple for debts incurred prior to their marriage. If you owned property or it was given or bequeathed to you before your marriage, it is not subject to seizure for payment of debts incurred by your husband before marriage. But this is because it is separate property. Rules regarding community property depend on the state. In Washington and Arizona, community property is subject only to community debt payments. Of course, when the community ends—as by death or divorce—and the property is separated, the share granted to a debtor or his estate can still be reclaimed by a creditor. In California and some other states, however, the earnings of a husband, which ordinarily would become community property, can be seized by his creditors for debts incurred prior to the marriage.

To illustrate the distinction regarding liability, if a husband endorses a promissory note for a friend, the lender generally cannot collect out of community property. But in the case of a lawyer who guaranteed the bail bond of a client, it was held that this was sufficiently related to his business, which provided the community property, to render the community property liable for seizure in payment of the debt.

If a wife is in business for herself and has had her husband waive his community property rights to her earnings (which is permitted in most, although not all, the community property states), the proceeds of her independent occupation are her separate property and are, of course, subject to debts she incurs. But remember that such agreements on the part of the husband should be in writing. In many instances they must be notarized.

The obligation to support a child of a previous marriage or a parent is generally considered separately from other debts or obligations voluntarily assumed, and can, therefore, be enforced against community property. However, your husband or his estate has to reimburse for this amount in the final division of the community property rights at divorce or death. In one California case, a court went as far as to say that a *wife's* mother, although ordinarily she could, if destitute, demand support from her child, cannot receive such support out of the community property of the wife. Yet, in another case, the *husband's* mother was put in a more favorable position, since the husband managed the community affairs. It would seem to be most acceptable for at least half of the community property to be subject to the claims of the dependents whose status was established by a relationship existing prior to the marriage. But it is not possible to generalize.

Sometimes, debts arise without any agreement on the part of the husband or wife. For example, suppose your husband operates his automobile negligently and is not adequately covered by liability insurance. Can the person he injures recover his judgment out of the community property entirely, out of only your husband's half, or not at all? The best ruling would seem to be that he can recover it out of your husband's share, but this rule is modified in different states. Accordingly, before you allow any creditor to seize any of the family estate, if you live in a community property state, check with a lawyer as to what immunities may apply. There may be many ramifications if a debt or obligation arose before marriage or while you were living in a non-community property state or if it is in connection with the separate investment or property of your husband.

We now approach the question of what happens to the community property in the event of death, divorce, or separation.

In many of the community property states the law provides that a wife who is living apart from her husband retains her own earnings free of community property claims where divorce occurs and a spouse is proved to be guilty of adultery or other flagrant misconduct. In some states, this is always the case, even without fault by the husband. In other respects, however, the termination of a marriage by divorce results in the partition of the community property and the delivery to the wife of only her share. Moreover, in some states, such as California, alimony may also be granted in addition to the share of community property.

If your husband dies, you take over the administration of your share of the community property. You do not inherit this half, you do not even "succeed" to it. You have always *owned* it and now merely assume the administrative rights of your husband which have terminated at his death. The disposition of the share of your deceased husband depends on his will. If your husband bequeaths one half of his entire estate to you, outright or in trust (see discussion of the marital deduction in chapter 9, "Inheriting It"), it may be advantageous to take under this bequest rather than community property. This is particularly so if he owned a great deal of "separate property" of which one half would come to you under the bequest, but not as community property. If he left no will, his property may pass by intestacy to be distributed according to the family situation. A few states limit the freedom of disposition by will of the share of community property belonging to the deceased spouse. Thus, it is well to be advised in advance on the laws of the community property state in which you live,

to be aware of your freedom—and your husband's freedom—of testamentary disposition of each share of the
community property. In New Mexico a surviving spouse
must inherit all the community property unless a portion of it has been set aside for the wife's support and
maintenance by a prior judicial decree.

It is interesting to note that if a couple has lived in a
community property state and the wife has achieved
certain community property rights and they then move
to a state, such as New York, which does not recognize
community property, a decree of divorce in the New
York courts would not have the power to change community property rights of either party with regard to
community property previously earned while the
couple was living in a community property state.

Permit us to reiterate our position about community
property. First of all, it is rarely understood by an
attorney who is not currently practicing in a community property state.

Also, the law of community property is evolving
very rapidly but at different paces in different community property states.

The whole trend is to diminish the husband's rights
and to put the woman on a parity with her husband
and to have *BOTH* as comanagers of the community
property as if it was jointly owned, rather than the old
rule which with few exceptions gave these rights exclusively to the husband.

However, it is impossible to detail for each of the
community property states how far the advance toward
joint control has proceeded, since, by the time this book
is published, in a given state, the law may have evolved
further than it has been in the past.

Accordingly, women in community property states,
as well as women who are moving into or out of such
states, should be sure that they are brought up to date
by a competent attorney practicing in that state.

Therefore, the statements made here should be looked
at as exemplary, and not as gospel.

The interpersonal decisions of a couple as to who is going to manage the property which belongs to both of them can be as important as the legal principles and may, in fact, modify, by agreement, what might otherwise be the legal position.

Accordingly, a married woman should always be aware that some act on her part or omission to act may still strongly affect her legal rights.

14

Selecting Your Financial Professional Advisers

Now that you have read through this book, you will realize that at some time or another, you will almost certainly have to seek the help of one or more types of professionals.

If this book helps you to pick a good accountant, a good lawyer, a good insurance agent, a good investment adviser, and the like, it will have performed, in this way alone, a most valuable job.

The lack of good professional help can undo everything that you or your husband or father or mother may have accomplished over a period of many months and even more. We have seen many cases where poor professional advice has wasted the fruit of half a lifetime of hard work.

If your family has a net taxable estate of $100,000 and $100,000 in life insurance (all figures are after all credits and exemptions), and if the insurance is not held in a trust for the benefit of the surviving wife or husband and for the children, it will become taxable. If you and your husband between you earn as much as

$30,000 a year, it will take you and your husband twenty-seven months to earn enough money to make up for the unnecessary estate tax on this insurance, *if you spend not one penny on your family and yourself and devote your entire income making up for this tax blunder.*

If you have a net taxable estate of $250,000 and $200,000 of insurance (above credits) and don't immunize the insurance from estate taxation, and you and your husband between you are earning $40,000, you will have to work fifty-two months to make up for this tax blunder.

Would you rather spend a few hours reading this book and a few hours with an estate planner or attorney rather than wasting twenty-seven or fifty-two months of work?

Recently, I talked to a widow whose husband had selected a notoriously ineffective trust company and gave no right to his widow to change the trust company. In April 1977, a financially-oriented friend of the widow wrote to the trust company suggesting a shift from one type of security, which was deemed totally inappropriate for the situation, into another type (in this instance, the recommended shift was from common stock into tax-free municipals, but this is certainly not always the appropriate thing to do for everyone. It appeared to be the appropriate thing to do for this widow at that time). The trust company refused to comply with the request and by June 1977, the common stocks had gone down 20 percent and the municipals had gone up 20 percent. The widow then took action before the probate judge, who ordered the trust company to comply with the recommendations, but by that time the losses had already been suffered and the widow had the personal strain and the expense of going to court. *One sentence added to the will by her husband (giving the widow the right to change trustees) could have avoided this kind of loss.*

In a divorce agreement, there is a provision for

alimony which is fair for today. However, the agreement does not contain a provision for cost-of-living adjustment. It is almost certain that with inflation, which comes sooner or later, this wife will be living in poverty before the end of her life. *One sentence added to the divorce agreement giving the wife the right to go back to the court or before an arbitration board for a cost-of-living adjustment would have avoided penury for the wife in her old age.*

An ineffective investment adviser can bankrupt you in a few months.

In all cases with all professionals, it is well to get references either among your own circle of friends or from someone to whom the prospective professional adviser can refer you. This is not an affirmative test. It is only a negative test. A professional may have all kinds of wonderful references and still turn out to be totally inadequate, but unless the professional can give you good references and unless you can talk to them in advance, stay away.

Also, in the case of all professionals, it is essential that there is individual rapport. This does not mean that you necessarily have to find the professional highly likable and someone you would like to invite to your home, but it does mean if his or her professional manner grates on you, you had better go to someone with whom you feel you can work both comfortably and effectively.

The most difficult problem in selecting a professional is the question of time. Almost always the competent and successful professional will have such an active clientele that he or she may not have the time to spare. Clear this up in advance. Inquire how much time your matters will probably involve and make sure that the professional not only has that time to spare, but that it will be available for you without waiting weeks for an appointment. If, when you call for your first appointment, you are informed that you cannot be seen for three weeks or more, go to someone else, except if the delay is because of illness or a vacation. If such delays occur on a first appointment, they almost always will occur repeatedly.

Also, when you are in conference with the professional, observe how many telephone or intercom communications are accepted by the professional. Sometimes a professional simply cannot avoid all interruptions. There are some crises which require interrupting a conference with a client. But we have never been able to understand why someone who picks up a telephone should be given a priority over another person who may have traveled a considerable distance for a personal interview. So, if there are more than one or two interruptions, or if the professional chats away on the telephone in a fashion that suggests that the interruption is not an absolute crisis, stay away from that professional. Moreover, if there is an interruption, the professional should explain to you in general terms, without revealing confidences or names, the nature of the interruption and why it was necessary.

Generally, it is a good idea to know in advance what the costs of the service of a professional will be, or at least the basis of determining those costs.

In some instances, the costs are on a time basis. If so, you should be told what the time rate is and be given an estimate of the number of hours that will have to be allotted to your problem. However, on many occasions, time is not an adequate measure of the fee. A brilliant attorney can come up sometimes with a solution to a costly problem in thirty seconds of time. But, those thirty seconds may reflect years of study and involvement. In such instances, effect should be given to the importance of the subject matter, the amount involved, and the results achieved, as well as the standing in the profession of the particular professional that you are consulting. A professional should not be penalized because the professional is able to get results in less time than others in the same profession.

Do not go shopping around for the lowest fee. This

does not mean that you should disregard expense, but you should not make it the final criterion of your choice. "The most expensive gun is the cheap one that doesn't fire when you pull the trigger." This does not mean that you should submit to extortionate fees, however. So, it may pay to make comparisons, but if you do, consider all the factors.

Sometimes, cases are handled on a "contingent" basis. This means that the professional's payment depends on the results accomplished. Usually in accident cases, the lawyer is paid a percentage of the settlement or verdict. Again, with a top expert a high percentage may turn out to be less expensive in the long run than a lower percentage from a person with less ability. In some cases, the professional will operate on a basis which is partially contingent. This means that the aggregate payment will be covered by the results accomplished but that a retainer or minimum will be required.

If the situation is such that it is impossible to fix a fee in advance, and it doesn't call for a contingent arrangement, the next attempt is to get a floor and ceiling on the charge, that is, a statement that the charge will be no less than a certain amount and no more than some other certain amount.

In some cases, it would be totally impossible to fix the fee in advance and then you must decide, based largely on the experience of other people with this professional, whether you trust the professional enough to put your affairs in the professional's hands, and whether you can also trust that professional enough to charge you a fair fee. Usually, a professional society will intervene if a fee is extortionate, and you can always refuse to pay and have the court decide the matter.

Some people like to be billed monthly or quarterly, others prefer paying a retainer and waiting until the matter has been completed before paying the balance of the fee. This is a matter of individual choice on the part of yourself and the professional.

Go to your professional as early in the problem as possible. Don't wait until after your tax return has been audited to go to your accountant or tax attorney for relief against a large deficiency proposed by the revenue agent. If we are talking about your taxes for 1982, you shouldn't go ahead blithely until April 1, 1983 and only then give your accountant a chance to prepare your tax return on a rush basis. Go to your tax planner, be it a tax lawyer or an accountant, in the fall of 1981, or even earlier, to prepare how to handle your tax situation for the ensuing year.

In estate planning, don't wait until you are fifty, sixty, or seventy. Start this in your late twenties, thirties, or, at the very least, your early forties. Don't wait unil you have taken a job before you have a tax lawyer and insurance agent check out the fringe benefits that go with the job.

As time goes by, check on whether the professional keeps in touch with you as to new principles affecting your situation.

If your professional has written books or magazine articles in professional magazines or newspapers on questions in his or her profession, read them. Even if they may be too complex for you to follow, you should at least be able to get some idea as to the imagination of the professional's approach to your type of problem.

With all professionals, see whether there is a backup (not necessarily in the same firm) in case the professional is out of town or ill or dies.

We shall now discuss some of the most important types of professional advisers to whom you may have to turn. To avoid any suggestion that one type of adviser is more important than the other, or more given to error than another, we shall discuss them in alphabetical order.

ACCOUNTANTS

There are three types of "accountants" to whom you

may turn. The first is a friend or fellow employee who has no more than bookkeeping training. The second is called a public accountant. This is someone who spends most of his or her professional time in accounting work, but who is not "certified." The third type is a CPA, which stands for "certified public accountant." In almost all states, this means that the accountant has taken a rigorous series of examinations offered by his or her state government or some agency or commission designated for this purpose. This represents, or should represent, the highest level of professional training and competence. Some CPA's are members of their state society of CPA's. Some are members of the American Institute of Certified Public Accountants.

In a large accounting firm, certain individuals are junior accountants, some are senior accountants, and some are partners. In addition to all these, there are professional people who do nothing but prepare income tax returns. Sometimes these people are well trained and well supervised and do a good job. Sometimes the reverse is true. In any event, they come in only *AFTER* the event and do not offer tax advice.

Do you need an accountant?

It seems to us that however moderate your income may be, you should at least go to some friend with bookkeeping experience or to a professional tax adviser. It is almost always the case that the latter, the professional tax return preparer, will save as much as the fee. The Internal Revenue Service does provide agents who will assist you in preparing your return, but it hardly can be expected that they will go out of their way to save you taxes. Remember, your tax is the result of four different factors: what you receive, what you spend, and various exemptions and credits.

If the family income grosses at $20,000 or more, you should go at least to a public accountant and, preferably, to a CPA.

If you get up to $50,000 or above, it usually pays to have the advice of a tax attorney and a CPA.

Don't rely on the accounting department of a large corporation for whom you may work. They may help you as a favor, but it can turn out to be a very costly one.

If you move into a community property state, or out of a community property state, you should consult a tax lawyer. Community property law is very intricate, and even if you move from one community property state to another, there are usually enough differences in the community property law from state to state to warrant engaging an attorney with specialized tax knowledge.

How do you select a CPA?

First of all, your selection should be based on the individual who will be handling your account. A firm may be one of the largest in the country, but you might find yourself assigned to an underling who doesn't have as much skill as an individual CPA whom you might consult. This is not to suggest that large firms are not appropriate. It is intended to emphasize that you should make your judgment not on a firm basis, but on the individual in the firm who is going to handle your affairs.

It is most important that your accountant have an inquiring and imaginative mind. Let the accountant look at some of your past tax returns and see if the accountant can come up with some suggestions as to how your tax affairs and the tax return could have been more effectively handled.

Make sure that your accountant has a good library which is kept up to date. The accountant should have a loose-leaf service which has all the current decisions and rulings and legislation in it. The accountant should also have basic textbooks on accounting and taxation. Inquire of the kind of current library the accountant has and what kind of back library he has. Unless the library has several hundred books in it, it is not adequate.

Check whether the accountant attends seminars on

specialized accounting problems related to your business, or tax seminars. Check whether your accountant is asked to participate in seminars on accounting and taxation. This is not conclusive in itself, however, since it might reflect nothing more than a good PR function; but if it exists, it is a plus factor.

ESTATE PLANNERS

This might be dubbed a new profession. Estate planning involves mathematics, tax law, knowledge of insurance, and considerable understanding of human nature.

A great many people are doing estate planning who have no business doing it. In many instances, estate planning is undertaken by insurance agents who piously end up by saying that you should review the recommendations with your attorney. But suppose your attorney is just a business attorney or a litigation attorney? An insurance agent, backed up by a good insurance company, is an indispensable ingredient of estate planning, but so is a tax lawyer, and frequently, a good accountant. In most of the very large law firms, they have one department drawing wills and trusts and another doing estate planning. Sometimes one department doesn't talk to the other one.

The first thing you should do is to reread chapter 9, "Inheriting It," and chapter 7 on life insurance, and see how many of the recommendations made there are mentioned by the estate planner. If the estate planner does not suggest the creation of a living trust, that is, a trust created during your lifetime, then, unless your estate, including all life insurance, whether supplied by your employer or not, is less than $200,000, this is a very bad indicator. Even if your estate is under $200,000, including insurance, if you have children or other dependents besides your spouse, a trust should be suggested. In many family situations, the smaller the estate the more important it is to save what you have.

Trusts perform many functions other than tax saving. If your estate planner does not suggest a living trust so that the trust can be moved from one state to another, that estate planner is tying your family to one location. Unless the estate planner recommends that either your surviving spouse, some other member of your family, or some friend have the right to change the trustee, you are not getting good advice.

Ask the prospective estate planner who should own the life insurance in your family. If he does not recommend that it be held by a trust, steer clear of that estate planner, unless your estate is under $200,000 *and you have no children or other dependents*.

Ask the estate planner what the virtues of a living trust may be. Compare his answers with the list of twenty-nine purposes of living trusts given at the very end of chapter 9. If the estate planner fails to mention at least two thirds of them, go elsewhere.

Ask the estate planner whether he or she is an attorney or works with an attorney. If the answers are negative, steer clear. Usually an attorney alone cannot do an adequate estate planning job unless he or she is also an insurance agent and an accountant, but an attorney is an indispensable ingredient of an estate planning job.

See how much time the estate planner devotes to analyzing the nature of the assets and liabilities in your estate, whether the estate planner checks out the fringe benefits, if any, offered by your employer, or suggests that you incorporate and have your own fringe benefits. Notice how much time is given to discussing your personal objectives.

If the estate planner does not ask about the wealth of your parents, in-laws, or other relatives from whom you may inherit, the job is not being done well.

Usually a financial statement, such as that found in chapter 6, "Borrowing It," or something similar to it, is essential, and an analysis of the family life insurance is also essential. Frequently, these things have been done by a competent insurance agent. If this has not been done by an insurance agent, and is not required by the estate planner, you should get another insurance agent or another estate planner (frequently the estate planner will just ask the questions and make up his or her own financial statement. It is not essential that you make it up. You should either make it up or supply the information, so that the professional can work with it).

If the age and emotional and financial maturity of your children are not discussed by the estate planner, go elsewhere.

Let us close by saying that the estate planner should know all or most of the things discussed in chapter 9.

INSURANCE AGENTS

Insurance agents are generally not given the recognition which they deserve. They perform an essential function in stirring up activity in the area of estate planning. The selection should be made from an independent agency system, that is, an agency which can acquire the best policy from the best company. This is far superior to a "captive" insurance agent who is required to offer any insurance business to a given company and may not go to another insurance company (which may have a better policy for your situation) unless his or her own company has turned down the business.

Note how thoroughly he or she analyzes your existing insurance. Note how extensively and precisely the insurance agent lists not only your own assets but those of your immediate family and, to the extent available, the assets of your parents or in-laws.

Determine the number of years the agent has been in business. All too often, the insurance business is the last retreat of someone unsuccessful in other occupations.

Note how many seminars on insurance, estate planning, and taxes the agent attends, or is invited to address.

Look for capability and grasp of mathematics, but don't permit the agent to dazzle you with a lot of numbers you don't understand. If you don't understand, ask the agent to explain, and be sure that the explanation makes sense.

Discuss the agent's thoughts and procedures and avoid the initial discussion of the particular insurance policy or company the agent is associated with. Life insurance is a tool supplying the results that are needed by a comprehensive financial and estate plan. Most such planning takes time and cannot be suggested, and should not be suggested, in the initial encounter, as a general rule.

Inquire who should own the policies and why. Compare the answers with the comments in chapter 9, "Inheriting It."

Ask the agent about the relationship between insurance and trusts and how trusts can be used both to hold and finance insurance. If the agent doesn't come up with most of the twenty-nine purposes of trusts mentioned at the end of chapter 9, or if the agent doesn't take you to an estate planner, go elsewhere.

In asking for references, particularly ask for references with accountants and attorneys. But be careful on this score because sometimes the accountant or attorney may be biased because the agent refers a lot of professional business to the accountant or attorney.

Carefully read chapter 8 on life insurance, and check out what is written there. Particularly ask about the comparative virtues and defects of both term and permanent insurance, and compare the responses with the comments on this subject in the aforementioned chapter on insurance.

Avoid an agent who too quickly agrees with your arguments. Being both agreeable and professional do not often go hand and hand.

It is difficult to ever obtain the best company. There are large varieties of methods of comparison, but make sure that your agent demonstrates to you what the comparative net costs over a period of at least twenty years (except if you are already seventy or more) will be. Remember that the same amount of insurance can have, over a period of years, twice as much cost with one company as with another. The data on insurance companies and their costs can be found in the publications of A. M. Best, which every agent should have.

Ask about the comparative virtues and defects of a mutual insurance company and stock company, and compare with our comments on insurance.

If a mutual company is being discussed and great emphasis is given to large dividends, ask the agent to go back ten or twenty years and compare the dividends actually paid with those that had been projected by the company. Ask the agent what is the best use of these dividends. If the agent doesn't suggest that they be used to purchase paid-up insurance, you probably do not have a top pro. Read the comments on this subject in the chapter on insurance.

Remember that the selection of a good insurance agent can represent the difference between penury and comfort for those whom you love.

INVESTMENT CONSULTANTS

Determine through personal interview the experience of the investment adviser handling your account.

Ask the consultant's technique for handling your money, that is, whether he uses technical, fundamental, or economic analysis.

Technical handling means trying to outguess the stock market and calculating whether the market is going up or down, depending on numerous factors such as the number of purchases and sales as related to whether the market went up or down. Too much reliance on this can be fatal.

Fundamental means going out into the field and personally analyzing and selecting particular companies for both their stability and growth possibilities. If this is not done by the investment analyst, or someone with whom the analyst works, steer clear.

Economic analysis means examination of the state of the national and world economy. Frequently, it is better to buy when the economy is down and to sell when the economy is up. The nature of the economy certainly should be studied, but in the end, it is the fundamental research, and the merits of the particular company and industry, which are the most important.

Determine for yourself whether the goals of the consultant are similar to your goals. Do you need income or growth of capital? In the *New York Times* of July 30, 1978, it was stated that Harvard University (whose results among the great institutions are second only to Stanford University of California) had switched from emphasis on growth to income; yet one of your authors, fourteen years previously, in his chapter on the stock market in *What Every Woman Doesn't Know* made the same recommendation.

Get the opinion of your accountant, attorney, insurance agent, or stockbroker.

Questions to ask your investment consultant are:
> *How much money do I need?*

Unless you have $25,000 of investable funds, very few will have anything to do with you. Some demand more.

> *What are my investment goals?*

One type of investment adviser is appropriate. If you are looking to maximize returns, choose one type. If you are looking for maximum safety, try another type, and for flexibility, you may need a third.

> *How important is the investment adviser's research organization?*

Not very. The best money managers work for themselves. Large organizations have several. There are exceptions. Investment companies should have funds left over to reward excellent money managers. Those who succeed in large organizations frequently leave to start their own firms. There are exceptions to this rule. One or two stockbrokerage firms have excellent research available, and a very few mutual funds can offer this. These sources may be particularly helpful if the amount available for investment is too small for the investment adviser you might otherwise select.

Should the investment adviser invest with me?

We support that type of investing. We find that investment advisers who have their own money invested in a pooled fund with clients tend to act more in the client's interest for obvious reasons.

Should I request a personal interview?

Absolutely. Demand to see records and client references. Satisfy yourself that the approach he is taking is the one you want.

Should I retain some control?

It is best not to. We suggest regular meetings in order to determine how the money manager is handling your funds, and whether it is in the manner which you both set up.

What sort of records should I receive?

Generally accepted are monthly statements. Feel free to discuss your investment adviser's excessive trading, or any particular transaction that he or she has made.

Should I rely on reputation?

Many money managers are hot or have a hot streak during periods of time. They seek out newspaper publicity in order to capitalize on their near-term record. Often they get favorable press and use that to back up accounts such as yours. Look beyond and ask to see records of prior results. Do not rely on reputation at the expense of your own personal investments.

What if my strategy is different from my money

manager's after a period of time? For example, what if I turn positive and he turns negative, or the reverse?

Pull your money out immediately. You and you alone are ultimately responsible for your money. It is not easy to work with someone who is opposed to your own views.

We suggest that you ask a prospective investment consultant how he or she goes about evaluating a given stock and deciding whether or not to buy or sell it and when to make such a move. The answers should be compared with the ten cardinal points in stock selection found in chapter 9, "Investing It." Unless most of these points are covered, we suggest you look elsewhere.

LAWYERS

This depends on what kind of attorney you are looking for.

We here discuss tax attorneys, business attorneys, and litigation attorneys.

Tax Attorneys

Here, it is very important to read books or articles written by the attorney or determine how many seminars the attorney addresses, and if possible attend such seminars.

Ask the attorney what his ideas are about wills and trusts and compare the responses to the material found in chapter 9, "Inheriting It." Particularly ask the attorney about the uses to which a living trust can be applied and check out how many of the twenty-nine purposes enumerated in chapter 4 are mentioned.

It is not necessary that the attorney should have had experience as an employee of the Internal Revenue Service. Sometimes this helps, but just as often it limits the thinking of the tax attorney.

Ask how he would recommend that you invest in the

business of some friend or relative, and check out his answers against the comments on 1244 corporations, Subchapter S corporations and partnerships, as mentioned in chapter 5, "Lending It." If the tax attorney flunks this test, go elsewhere.

See if you can arrange to be on a moderately priced annual-retainer basis so that planning is done well in advance.

It is not necessary that a tax attorney have actual accounting experience. In fact, this can have negative results, since accountants are supposed to record facts as they are, while tax lawyers should see that your affairs are ordered as they should be. An accountant looks primarily at the past, and a tax lawyer should look primarily to the future.

The same comments that were mentioned earlier about the professional's library and current loose-leaf service apply to tax lawyers.

The tax attorney should have either a daily or at least weekly service that keeps him or her up to date.

Tax law is one of the most complicated functions of the law. Tax aspects are mentioned throughout this book. Before you engage a tax lawyer, or continue with a tax lawyer whom you have already retained, go back over this entire book and check out the attorney's attitudes and recommendations in comparison with what is written here.

Business Attorneys

This is an attorney who writes contracts, keeps corporate minutes, and works on real estate transactions.

If the business attorney also has considerable tax skills, as they are described above, this is extremely helpful. If the business attorney does not have tax skills, ask the business attorney what tax lawyer the business lawyer works with. If the answer is "no one in particular," go elsewhere. If your prospective attorney mentions a specific name or firm, check out the same as indicated above, regarding top lawyers.

This is an area where it is so hard to lay down specific criteria that reference to clients who have been with the attorney for some years are particularly important.

It would be helpful if the attorney could show you a typical contract he had drawn, but it is difficult to do this without violating personal confidential relations. On the other hand, if you are recommended to a business attorney by a friend, ask the friend to show you contracts drawn. Inevitably, these contracts will have some legal jargon in them which will be difficult for you to follow, but the question is how much. At least, you should be able to understand most of the contract easily.

It is also important with this type of attorney that you endeavor to arrange an annual retainer so that you will be induced to check matters with the business attorney before you get too thoroughly enmeshed in a difficult situation.

Litigation Attorneys

Inquire into the field of law in which the attorney specializes. If it is indicated that this was in trial work, inquire what percentage of the practice involved litgation.

Also inquire what type of litigation. Some litigation lawyers specialize in patents, others in accident cases, and so on. If the response is that the lawyer works in general litigation, nevertheless check out how much experience the attorney has had with your particular type of problem.

Inquire about the length of time that the attorney has been practicing and how many trials are handled per year. Also, how many were brought to a conclusion and what the philosophy regarding settlement is, and whether the attorney usually settles at the time of trial or prior thereto. We have found that all too often lawyers are prone to settle matters too quickly. While it is true that "a bad settlement is better than a good lawsuit," nevertheless, the best way to get a *good* settlement is to expect to go to trial and prepare as early as possible, through depositions or examinations before trial of the opposing party and key witnesses, to get all of the facts in the case. The more ready you are to go to trial, the more probable it is that you will get an early and good settlement.

Does the attorney use investigative services or perhaps have an employee who is an investigator? What is the attorney's philosophy about taking depositions and examination before trial, filing motions for disclosure, discovery, and so on? What practice is followed about making an attachment through a prejudgment remedy, that is, tying up the opponent's assets at the commencement of the action? Obtain a careful explanation about the type of case in which this can be done. Does the attorney generally try cases before the court, namely, a judge, or before a jury? If before a jury, an attorney's manner, decorum, personality, and speaking ability are important factors. If possible, observe a prospective attorney in action.

Does the attorney maintain adequate communications with the client and send copies of correspondence and pleadings to the client? Is the attorney reachable by telephone? In this field, the availability of time from the attorney, as discussed in our statement of general principles, is particularly vital. While it was stated above that an attorney should be loath to accept telephone interruptions during a conference with a client, it also follows that if you call and your attorney is in conference you should expect a call-back during the same day or, at the least, during the next business day, or if not that, you get a very good excuse for the neglect. If your lawyer takes too long to reach you, either in person or by phone, go elsewhere.

Is the attorney interested in the client's opinion and in periodic consultations with the client?

Does the attorney send a case update report periodically?

Does the attorney try cases for other lawyers who are not trial lawyers and can references be given to such referral lawyers for whom litigation matters are handled? Inquire whether, if the case is lost, the lawyer would be willing to take it up on appeal.

Does your prospective attorney handle appeals?

Nothing runs up fees like litigation, and here it is particularly important to discuss fees in advance as suggested above.

REAL ESTATE

The choice of a real estate broker can be crucial both in investment in real estate and the sale of real estate.

While the sale of real estate is not exactly the converse of its purchase, it has been our experience that a broker who is good at buying real estate is also, almost certainly, good at selling it, since she is able to enumerate the aspects of the property that would be attractive if *she* represented a buyer.

The number of years in the business is important. They certainly should not be less than two and more often at least five years.

The number of sales or purchases made during the current year or the prior year is very important. There should be a substantial purchase or sale every month, except if the broker has been ill or away on vacation. The total amount of the value of property purchased or sold should be at least $1,000,000 a year.

References from satisfied customers are particularly useful in this area, since one situation is more apt to be like another situation than in the case of law, accountancy, and the like.

Connections with other offices in the immediate community, in surrounding communities, and access to offices of brokers in all parts of the country are very important, particularly if you find that you need to buy or sell some property thousands of miles away.

The broker's standing with the banks in this case is very important, particularly since mortgage financing is frequently necessary in purchasing property.

When you are buying a house, the broker should be asked what points he or she would consider important information for the buyer before purchase. The real estate broker's criteria should include:

1. If possible, executives of the school system and the principal of the particular school the children will attend should be interviewed. The quality of the faculty and the size of the classes in relation to the number of the faculty should be checked out. The standing of the school in various rating systems should be checked out.

The recreational facilities of the area, particularly the availability of beaches and swimming pools, should be verified.

The mill rate, that is, the rate of real estate taxation in relation to the value of the property should be checked out. In some cases, the assessment of the value of the property is only a portion of its fair market value and this should be verified.

It is also important to discover whether the town has some recently acquired debt for a special facility such as a new high school or whether there is anticipated a substantial increased indebtedness, which will have the effect of increasing the taxes.

The applicability of some law or constitutional mandate, such as that adopted in the first half of 1978 under the famous "Proposition Thirteen" in California should be examined.

The credit standing of the particular unit of government, be it town or city or county, should be checked with a stockbrokerage firm active in the underwriting and sale of tax-exempt securities.

The zoning laws should be analyzed, and consideration should be given as to whether they are so harsh that they are likely to be upset in the courts. This should be verified with local attorneys. Frequently when zoning regulations are too harsh, there is a shift to the other extreme.

The distance between the property and major transportation facilities and thruways and freeways should be verified, as well as the distance from schools and shopping facilities.

The number of policemen and volunteer or professional firemen per capita of population should be known.

The number of residents per square mile should be checked out, and the rate at which this ratio is increasing or decreasing tested out.

The presence of low-income housing should be examined. Unfortunately, this frequently tends to lessen the value of other property.

The building and environmental requirements of the town should be known, and an inspection by appropriate inspectors in these areas should be updated.

If the broker doesn't consider these points important and come up with most of these answers, look elsewhere for another broker.

If you are selling property, multiple listing with all the brokers in a multiple-listing system should be considered, but it is important that the listing, whether multiple or not, provide that no bid has to be accepted by the vendor and that the listing can be canceled at will. It is not wise to give an exclusive and particularly an exclusive noncancelable listing, unless the real estate broker is so extraordinary that it is deemed worthwhile to accept these dangerous limitations.

If the broker is part of a franchise, careful consideration of this factor should be made. One advantage of franchising is that the availability of listings in other parts of the country may be increased, but it may be that your nonfranchised broker has equally effective avenues, or it may be that the franchise system doesn't operate too well in the exchange of opportunities between franchised offices. Usually, the franchisor deducts as much as 8 percent of the commissions, and it is important that the franchise holder clearly demonstrate the advantages of dealing with her.

In choosing a sales broker rather than a purchasing broker, the following special considerations should be kept in mind.

1. Her rate of compensation. Sometimes the commission can be reduced. Sometimes it is not wise to expect this with an exceptionally efficient broker.
2. The amount of advertising which will be done by the broker and samples of prior advertising should be reviewed.
3. The rest of the factors are more or less the same as with a purchasing broker.

If you are engaging a broker to acquire undeveloped land as an investment, the same questions as with a home should, in general, be asked, but more attention should be given to zoning and environmental regulations.

Also, the developments in the price at which undeveloped real estate has been sold should be considered.

It is also important that the broker advise you that an engineer should examine the property, unless this has already been done in the process of obtaining subdivision and building permits.

If you are looking to acquire improved commercial real estate, the broker should list the following information as being important, as a test of whether or not to use her services.

1. The age of the building or buildings should be noted.
2. The number of acres still available for additional building is of critical importance. This

is because building on this extra space can be an inflation hedge.

3. The terms of the leases should be thoroughly examined.

4. Parking requirements and facilities are important.

5. The cost of the building in terms of square footage should be examined and compared with the current construction costs, while allowing for depreciation.

6. The rents stipulated are of particular importance, and in view of inflation it is generally important to have the rents be a minimum guarantee with provision of percentage overage if sales go above a certain figure. This is an escalation clause.

7. Renewal options should be examined.

8. The operating expenses experienced should be examined, even though you might have net leases where all the expenses must be paid by the tenant.

9. The mortgage terms should be reviewed carefully.

10. The broker should verify whether and how much of a mortgage the vendor will take back and on what terms.

11. The competition of other commercial space should be examined.

12. The "lead store" is of critical importance, and the financial and merchandising efficiency of that tenant should be verified.

13. The cost of insurance on the property should be checked.

14. Also, the cost of utilities should be checked.

15. It should be checked whether the net leases provide for both interior and exterior repairs.

Similar types of questions as to office buildings and industrial buildings should be checked out with the broker. Ask her what are the important elements and see how she passes this test.

STOCKBROKERS

The selection of a stockbroker is of less or greater importance depending on whether or not you can afford and have selected a good independent investment adviser.

Generally, a stockbroker should either specialize in one particular aspect of the market, such as commodities, municipal bonds, or the like, or should have a particular comprehensive financial coverage of every aspect of investment, including tax shelters, which should not be purchased without a separate review by a tax attorney.

If you cannot afford an investment adviser, and the price of an attractive mutual fund (see chapter 4, "Investing It") is too high, the best place to go is to a good stockbroker.

It is particularly helpful if you have prior experience in investing on your own through an investment club, and it is important that you have time and enough interest to subscribe to several financial periodicals, such as those mentioned in the "Investing It" chapter.

The experience of executives of the firm is very important, but you should verify that you will be dealing with the same individuals as those who pin a gold medal on the brokerage firm.

The education and training of the account executive who will be handling your account, and of their research people, is very important.

The fashion in which a stockbroker executes orders is very important whether or not you have independent investment counsel. The difference of a quarter of a point in the execution of either buy or sell orders can, over the years, add up to a fortune. However, their effectiveness can be judged only by actual experience. On buy orders you might check how close their purchase was for the "low" of the day in the stock market reports, and on sell orders you might check how close it was to the "high" of the day.

The salaries, bonuses and fringe benefits paid to these people are also important. If not adequate, the good ones will be tempted to go into business for themselves as investment advisers.

Many of the points mentioned with reference to investment advisers are obviously applicable to stockbrokers, such as whether or not their research people actually visit the companies in whose stock they are investing.

Most large brokerage firms have regular publications, and it would be well to read back publications and compare comments made and predictions offered to what happened later on.

The day of the fixed commission rate has gone. Commission rates should be checked. Many large brokerage firms give discounts to volume purchasers. While you cannot expect the same discount as a heavy volume purchaser, it is also the case that you will not expect as much service. The rate of commission is, therefore, something which should be discussed.

You should very carefully check at least monthly on the results you have obtained and at the end of the year compare the income and appreciation (or losses) with the commissions paid by your account. Sometimes, you may find out that the stockbroker has made more money with the capital than you have. On the other hand, do not begrudge the broker a commission, particularly if the results indicate that it has been well earned.

It is not a particularly good idea to scatter your account between several brokers. If you concentrate with one broker, you will deserve and should receive better treatment.

If you talk to an investment consultant who impresses you favorably, but then discover your account is too small, the investment consultant will probably be

274 Money and Women

able to recommend you to a good stock brokerage firm anyway.

Be sure that your broker discusses with you the appropriate investment philosophy and ascertain whether you are comfortable with the philosophy of the broker.

TRUSTEES

Get the following information, preferably in writing or through your attorney:

How many years of experience has the trust department?

What is the present cost and/or market value of trustee investments?

What percentage of the investments is in real estate, corporate bonds, municipals, mortgages, stocks, other equities, etc.?

Where are your trust offices located?

What is the number of employees in administration, in investment, in operations?

What are your fees? Are they fixed by law, or can we negotiate about them? Are there extra charges?

Do you handle investment research within the trust department? With correspondent banks? Through outside advisers?

Will you work with investment counsel designated by me or the beneficiaries, provided you are excused from responsibility if you follow the adviser's recommendations?

How do you assign the trust officer to my account? Do I have a choice now or later?

Where you have discretion in handling and distributing income and capital, what methods do you use in exercising such discretion?

How will you select the outside attorney doing the legal work on this trust?

How does your investment performance over the last five years compare with the Dow Jones averages,

S & P 500 results and other published results of trustee accomplishments?

If you have a group of small trust accounts, will you put them into a common fund? How many of such funds do you maintain and what are their special characteristics? What have been the results?

Will you supply me with a proposed portfolio of the changes you would immediately recommend in my existing holdings?

Will you examine Chapter 9, Inheriting It, in this book and advise whether you are in general sympathy with its principles.

Index

A

B

C

FREE
Fawcett Books Listing

There is Romance, Mystery, Suspense, and Adventure waiting for you inside the Fawcett Books Order Form And it's yours to browse through and use to get all the books you've been wanting . . . but possibly couldn't find in your bookstore.

This easy-to-use order form is divided into categories and contains over 1500 titles by your favorite authors.

So don't delay—take advantage of this special opportunity to increase your reading pleasure.

Just send us your name and address and 35¢ (to help defray postage and handling costs).